Call Me Eli

A GENDERQUEER MEMOIR

By Eli Michael Klyde

Cover image © Shutterstock.com

www.innovativeinkpublishing.com
Send all inquiries to:
4050 Westmark Drive
Dubuque, IA 52004-1840

Print ISBN: 979-8-3851-6433-2
eBook ISBN: 979-8-3851-6434-9

Published in the United States of America

For Darrian.

And for all those young people who feel like they'll never fit in.

Table of Contents

Acknowledgements

Thank you to my editor, Tiffany Brooks, for helping me make this memoir the best it could be. And thanks to my first readers–Lesli Bangert, Alaunde Copley-Woods and Matt Lubich–for ensuring me that this book was indeed something important and that I should keep working on it. Thanks to my very early writing partner, Julie Robinson, who encouraged me to pursue this project and let me know I needed to be more than a journalist explaining what happened but to also include the emotion behind the story. Finally, thank you to my partner, Sara Greenberg, for supporting me and letting me read the manuscript to you over and over.

About the Author

Eli Michael Klyde is a professor of journalism at the University of Northern Colorado in Greeley. Their work has appeared in the (Boulder) *Daily Camera*, *The Johnstown Breeze*, *The Denver Post*, The (Greeley) *Tribune*, the (Durham) *Herald-Sun*, and *The Connecticut Post*. When not cheering on the Boston Red Sox and the UConn women's basketball team, they try to live peacefully near Boulder.

Introduction

I *am a toddler*. It's sometime in the early '70s, and I am sitting in a small auditorium in New Haven, Connecticut. My babysitter is reading from a *Curious George* book while my mother is in a nearby room, talking with other women about liberation. It's fitting that this is my earliest memory. My mother's feminism would shape my life.

I am in first or second grade. Back then, we lined up a few times each day to visit the bathroom. We'd walk in our lines down the hallway until we reached the restrooms: one marked "boys," the other, "girls." I never really thought about going into the boys' room until someone dared me to enter. I failed to see what the challenge was.

"Lynn, did you get mixed up?" my teacher asked after retrieving me and redirecting me to the girls' room. No, I think to myself–now. But maybe even back then I understood something fundamental about myself, even though I wouldn't realize it consciously for many years.

I am eight years old. I am in ballet class. I'm not sure why I decided to take ballet. It might have been that an older neighbor girl whom I looked up to was doing it. The teacher tells me I walk like a farm boy. I leave early to get to baseball practice on time. As I grow up, I will consistently choose sports over other activities whenever I can.

I am a seventh grader and one of the top students in the class, so I have the privilege of helping at the eighth-grade graduation. My job is to stand at the door to the auditorium, playing sentry as the boys enter practice for the ceremony. We practice for several days, and each time certain boys pass, they growl jabs: "You gonna play football this year, Lynn?" When a teacher realizes what's happening, she moves me to the stage, where the boys are forced to be quiet. I still wonder why those boys felt the need to bully me, and why I never felt strong enough to push back.

I am fourteen years old. The year is 1982. It is the day of my Bat Mitzvah. I am wearing a beige dress with lacy trim. I feel out of place. Not quite myself.

I am seventeen. I am excited about my upcoming prom. I don't really like boys. I don't know yet that I will someday like girls, but I enjoy fantasizing about them while lying in bed at night. I don't think there's anything particularly wrong with this, and I certainly won't do anything about these thoughts for at least another decade. I just push them down, like all my feelings, and try to convince myself I am "normal."

I am in my late twenties. I am an out lesbian. I finally feel good about myself. I wear a crew cut and men's clothing. It feels right. But eventually I start acting and dressing more feminine again. I am not sure why. Maybe I am ashamed, though it's hard to figure out exactly why. I just know that I don't fit in the way I am "supposed" to.

I am fifty-six years old. I am wearing a tie. I am celebrating my new name. I am finally myself.

***

This is the story of a girl who grew up to be an adult who sometimes longs to be a boy. It's the story of a person who was very sick, very angry, and very sad for many years.

It's the story of how a mother's love, and her love of feminism, shaped me into the person I am today. It's the story of how my father's influence gave me not only a love for sports, but a passion for making the world a better place.

It's not a story about having all the answers, but about learning not to live in fear of the questions. It's the story of how a depressed, broken person eventually became healthy, happy and whole by learning to live honestly. It's a story about how this boi met themselves again for the first time.

1

Honoring my roots

A few years ago, I took one of those genetic tests and found out I'm about ninety percent Eastern European Jew. No surprise there. It's all in the genes, you might say.

I am who I am in large part because of my family of origin. And to call that family of origin odd would be an understatement.

My great-great-grandfather, Ben Fuchs, was bitten by a rabid dog and went mad in the bathtub, as the story goes. This happened in the old country, in a little village called Plinsk. We're not sure where it was exactly–possibly Poland or Russia or maybe even Belarus. I don't know if this story is true, but a fear of dogs was certainly passed down. Years ago, when I told my Aunt Goldie–my grandmother's sister–that I had a cat, she said she didn't like animals because of what had happened to her grandfather.

My mother's maternal grandmother refused to cook after her husband died. She ate out for lunch and dinner every day. She couldn't read English, so she would ask the waiter, "What's good today?"

A fistfight broke out between two of my cousins at another cousin's Bar Mitzvah. I'm pretty sure that alcohol played a large part in this ruckus. Like my cousins on this crazy night, I would eventually fall victim to the negative side of drinking, and it would affect my life profoundly.

The peculiar nature of my family was not lost on me. I have always been an odd duck. But I think understanding my relatives is more than merely seeing what we have in common. Maybe knowing where I came from can help me better understand why I did the things I did and felt the things I felt.

One of my great-grandmothers on my father's side spoke Yiddish all her life. Perhaps this is why I have compassion for folks who come to the United States and continue to speak their native languages. Sometimes I feel cheated that my grandparents didn't teach Yiddish to their children. I guess they wanted their kids to fit in, and at the time, the way to do that was to become fully "Americanized." This approach seemed to mean pretending like no memory of the old country existed.

***

My maternal grandmother was the only biological grandparent I ever knew. She met my grandfather at a Jewish family summer camp in the Catskills in the early twentieth century. My grandmother, born Clara Fox, had been hanging out with a boy all week, but when Friday came, he said he couldn't hang out with her that night.

"Why not?" she asked.

"You're not that kind of girl," he told her.

She sat on the porch swing rocking back and forth and feeling deeply hurt. A nice fellow happened to walk by and saw her, and they got to talking. When she got home to her apartment near the corner of 125th Street and Amsterdam Avenue in Manhattan, she was ironing when there was a knock on the door. It was Michael Klyde, "all the way from Brooklyn!" as my grandmother remembered it. And Michael Klyde from Brooklyn became my grandfather.

They honeymooned in Cuba, where they experienced a memorable incident Grandma described years later. They entered a club in Havana, and the man at the door asked, "How many?" My grandfather, not wanting to look stingy, answered "three," and gave the man what he assumed was their ticket price. Then, Grandma said, "three women came out with a bed."

"He grabbed the money, he grabbed me, and we ran out of there," she would tell me as we played cards in her condominium in Florida.

Clara came from money; her father was a furrier. Michael, nicknamed Mack, was raised in more meager circumstances. He would eventually own a linoleum store, but as my mother often said, because he did not deal in the black market during World War II, he never got rich. He worked hard, though, and the family was well off enough to afford to employ a housekeeper/nanny. Annie, a Black woman, had a great influence on my mom, and when Annie died years later, my mother mourned her beloved friend.

Grandma was born in 1905 and had some old-fashioned views on race and gender. Once, she saw a Black woman on the subway and asked her "Do you want to clean my house?" The woman deadpanned, "No, you wanna clean mine?" Many years later, when she was in her eighties, we were sitting on her porch when a neighbor walked by. "You know," her voice dropped to a whisper. "He's *gay*." I was not quite sure of my own sexuality at the time, so I didn't know how to respond to the shame she implied with her tone of voice.

Finally, I managed to mumble something like, "What's wrong with that?"

"It's in the Bible," she replied, as if that settled the matter once and for all. I could have pointed out that the spareribs she always ordered at the Chinese restaurant around the corner were made with pork, but I kept my mouth shut. Even as a grown-up, I would never argue with Grandma Clara.

Perhaps my grandmother's attitude toward homosexuality was one reason I stayed in the closet until I was twenty-six. I can only imagine what Grandma would think had she known her only granddaughter eventually married a woman. What would she make of the fact that I wear men's pants, a boy's shirt and a tie when I dress up? I'm actually laughing a little as I write this. But looking back, I always dressed like a boy when I was a child, and Grandma never seemed to have a problem with it. She didn't seem to have a problem with the fact that I was more into sports than dolls, either. Maybe I need to give her a little more credit. After all, she never did anything but love me dearly. She used to call me *sheyne leben*, a common expression in Yiddish for doting grandparents to say to little girls. It translates roughly to "pretty life." I've come to see myself as "handsome," rather than "pretty," but I think Grandma would understand.

I remember visiting her in Great Neck, Long Island, for a week every summer. She would take me to the city pool each day and let me have two Pepperidge Farm Lido cookies with a glass of milk each night before bed. Those treats–rich butter cookies with a thick layer of chocolate between–were always my favorites, and every time I think of them, I also think of Grandma Clara.

I remember visiting her in the condominium in Florida after she moved down there for good. And I remember playing casino and gin with her—her fingers, the knuckles gnarled from arthritis, shuffling the cards and making a bridge. She claimed the arthritis didn't cause her pain, but I still wonder.

My grandmother's love shaped me, as did her worldview. Her perspective on social issues certainly didn't jibe with mine, but she grew up in another time. I can still honor her memory despite the gap between our outlooks on the world.

***

I wish I could have known all my grandparents. My father's parents died when I was about three, and I have no memory of them.

Grandpa Mack had a heart attack at 50, then developed pancreatic cancer and died while my mother was in college. I don't know much about him. My mom used to tell me that every time Grandma Clara walked by, he would grab her behind. She also said he drank his tea out of a glass with a sugar cube between his teeth. I wish I knew more.

Grandma remarried a few years after Mack died. Ruben Krevat might have been my mom's stepfather, but he wasn't "step" anything to me. He treated me as if I were his biological grandchild. He took me fishing and tried to teach me golf, but he always said I swung the club like a baseball bat. When I became a Bat Mitzvah in 1982, he celebrated his second Bar Mitzvah at the same time. He was eighty-three, a traditional time for a second of these Jewish coming-of-age rituals. I'm glad Grandma was able to spend a quarter century with Grandpa Ruby; he was a good man.

Grandma Clara and Grandpa Mack had three kids–two girls and boy; my mother was the middle child. She was born in Brooklyn, but the family moved to Buffalo when she was young. Nevertheless, Grandma never let go of her identity as a Manhattanite. When the family went back to visit relatives in New York City, she also took them for new shoes at a shop on the ground floor of the Empire State Building. My mom always wanted to go up to the top, but my grandmother would tell her, "That's for tourists."

"We *were* tourists," my mother told me when she recounted that story years later.

My mother grew up in a universe vastly different from the one I experienced as a girl, yet we both struggled to find ourselves. My mother managed to do so much more quickly than I did, however.

She was one of those people who did not hold back her feelings about anything of which she disapproved—which happened to be quite a lot. Sometimes when I talked about my mother, my ex-wife would say, "Yes, but did she *like* anything?"

And it was true: She didn't like a lot of things. She hated Julie Andrews. (Who hates Julie Andrews?) She always said Andrews was "too sweet." She discouraged me from watching Andrews in *The Sound of Music* because it "made the Nazis into a joke." She detested *Hogan's Heroes* for the same reason.

She was blunt. She told people what she felt, often with little regard for their feelings. I remember her reaction when my son, then about six, scored in the 98th percentile on the gifted and talented test.

"Well, they include people from Mississippi in the results."

I'm not even sure what this was supposed to mean. But that wasn't the end of it.

"Is he gonna take a short bus to school?"

When I was a kid, "taking the short bus" implied that a child had a mental disability because the disabled kids rode to school in a different bus, which was about half the size of the regular bus.

I never confronted her about these comments, but they hurt me. I don't understand why she couldn't have just been happy for my son and me. Why did she have to attack?

I learned how to be critical from both my parents. I was like that for a long time. Today I'm more compassionate, but I often complain about things that most people would just let go, like mispronunciations by sportscasters and missing apostrophes in headlines, or when someone on a reality show I'm watching uses "me" when "I" is called for. I don't mean to criticize; it's just a kneejerk response because it was the normal reaction in my home to anything short of my parents' perceptions of perfection.

***

My mother pursued a master's degree in counseling as a young parent. She was a staunch feminist and refused to buy into social pressures that told her she should tamp down her ambitions or be defined by marriage and motherhood.

My father was as close to the vest as my mother was open about her opinions. I always knew he supported me, but we struggled to communicate in a way that the other understood. It wasn't just me, though; my parents never really got along. I only saw them hold hands once, and an eerie silence surrounded their relationship for as long as I can remember. I have a recurring nightmare that my parents are getting back together, and when I have the dream, I usually wake up screaming.

Despite the pain I remember from my childhood, it wasn't all bad. My brother and I had every material thing we needed, and there were many good times. Our parents loved us in their own ways, yet something was always missing.

My relationship with my mother was the most important one on my life, but I don't think I ever got that unconditional love that children expect from their parents. I just didn't understand how that shaped me until years later.

My parents at their engagement party. They were married in 1961 and split up in 1992.

Clockwise from left: my mother, my father, my paternal grandfather, my maternal grandmother, my paternal grandmother, and my brother, before I was born.

Grandma Clara holding me when I was wearing a body
cast. I was born with a broken hip and had to have it fixed
when I was very young.

My dad, me, my mom, and my brother sometime in the 1970s.

2

Hear her roar

As the plane lifted off, I prayed for two things:
"God, let her live until I get there." And, "Please don't let her suffer."
Two days earlier, I'd gotten a call from my brother, Geoffrey.
"Mom's in the hospital."

I can't say the news was a complete shock; my mother smoked for at least 30 years. She supposedly quit after suffering a heart attack in her late 50s, but 15 years later, her bedroom still reeked of smoke. She ended up with COPD (chronic obstructive pulmonary disease)—which includes emphysema and chronic bronchitis.

I asked her once if she had emphysema.

"I don't want to talk about it," was her only reply.

Mom had had a scare about eighteen months earlier and ended up on a respirator for a week. As soon as I heard about that first episode, I caught a plane to North Carolina — where she had settled after retirement. As I sat in the airport waiting for my connecting flight, I called Mom's best friend to tell her I was on my way.

"Oh." There was an awkward pause on the other end. "The first thing she said when she woke up was 'Whatever you do, don't tell my children.'"

Mom had made her best friend her emergency contact, so the only reason my brother and I found out about her intubation was the fact that when she didn't bring her newspaper in for several days, her neighbor called the hospital and found out, then called me.

When I got to the hospital, she was asleep. It was difficult seeing her hooked up to all those machines. She must have sensed that, too, because when she woke up, she made a little gesture with her hand, shooing me out of the room. I think she was embarrassed to have me see her like that. She always pretended to be tough, but I think deep inside, she was actually quite fragile.

I thought I was going to lose her during that first episode. After they took her off the ventilator, she had a setback. The pulmonologist gave it to me straight: Because of the COPD, she had trouble emptying her lungs of carbon dioxide. She also had a heart problem.

"When her lungs have trouble working, her heart can't compensate," the doctor said. "And when her heart has trouble working, the lungs can't compensate."

I called my brother, who was supposed to arrive the next day, and told him he'd better hurry up. But Mom pulled through. After that, she indicated "Do Not Resuscitate" on her advance directive. She said being on a respirator was too hard on the family.

A few months later, we celebrated her 75th birthday and the seemingly miraculous turnaround in her health.

Less than a year later, she caught a simple cold, which can be deadly for someone with COPD. When the doctor called me that Friday night to say it was time to come, I knew this was the beginning of the end.

And so, once again, I was sitting on a plane headed toward North Carolina, wondering if my mother was going to die, hoping to get there before it happened. Thoughts spun through my mind — all the fun we'd had together over the years; all the sorrows she'd endured during her lifetime; all the things I'd learned from her. And how she taught me what it meant to be a feminist.

My mother often bragged about the fact that I was breastfed at Women's League meetings. (And she always pointed out that she wasn't talking about the League of Women Voters; they weren't nearly radical enough for her tastes.) She swaddled me in feminism. I drank it in like breastmilk and relished what I learned from her.

Betty Friedan's *The Feminine Mystique* was published in 1963, two years after my parents married and a year after my older brother was born. Mom often remarked about the timing: "If I'd gotten married two years later, I wouldn't have changed my name."

What I think she was actually saying was that if she'd waited two years and read the book first, she'd never have gotten married in the first place. At least not to my father. In that way, perhaps feminism came a bit too late for her, but in many ways, it was right on time.

I'm not sure exactly what my mother did in the women's movement, but I remember it was a big part of her life in the 1970s. I think it involved a lot of consciousness-raising activities. I know she stopped shaving her legs for a while as a form of protest. And I know she gained a lot of self-esteem. She became her own woman, beholden to no one. When Mom got married, a women couldn't get a loan without her husband's permission. Yet when I was growing up, it was my mother who handled the household finances. She refused to be kept down by society's sexist traditions.

Despite her intelligence, she was told to be a teacher—something she never wanted to do—because, other than nursing and secretarial work, that was all there was for women when she graduated from high school in 1956. So she became a high school teacher after college and taught for a few years before marrying my dad and giving birth to Geoffrey. But after I was born six years later, she went back to school to earn a master's degree. She became a guidance counselor and retired as the director of guidance for an adult trade school. She was determined to help others achieve that same sense of liberation and independence that she had.

***

When I was young, my heroes were athletes like baseball star Roger Clemens and NFL Hall-of-Famer Lawrence Taylor. In college, I looked up to Martin Luther King Jr. and Bobby Kennedy for their work on civil rights. Later in life, I idolized athletes who broke barriers, like Martina Navratilova, Jackie Robinson, and Hank Greenberg. Yet when I truly rack my brain for a hero in my life, it's got to be my mom.

She was born in 1938 and was named after her maternal grandfather, Jacob Louis Fox. The tradition in many Jewish families is to name a child after a respected dead relative, using the namesake's first two initials. She was named June Lillian: "JL" for Jacob Louis. But when her brother was born three years later, her parents named him Jacob Louis. Mom always resented this. She cried when she told us about it much later in life.

"They gave my name away," she said, sobbing.

Patriarchy was nothing new in my family. My maternal grandmother was one of four children–two boys and two girls. The boys were named "Baruch Bernard" and "Baruch Moshe," which meant "Blessed Bernard" and "Blessed Moses." The girls were plain old "Clara" and "Goldie," as if they didn't deserve to be blessed.

The name thing really affected my mother. She felt as if she wasn't considered important because she was a girl. When she told us about the name issue, she also told us that she was changing her Hebrew name to *D'vorah*, which means "Deborah," after an aunt whom she dearly loved. Perhaps the loss of her initials is where her deep devotion to equality and justice came from. She passed that trait on to me. Maybe that's why I joined a lesbian activist group while in grad school. And why I share political posts on Facebook. And it's one of the reasons I went into journalism: I wanted to change things for the better. And maybe I'm doing that now by educating the next generation of journalists.

***

My mother was a bit imposing, both physically and emotionally. She was a tall woman (about 5'8") with a low voice. She wore her straight, dark brown hair relatively short and didn't bother much with make-up. She never dressed particularly fashionably, preferring clothing that was comfortable—especially when it came to footwear. When I was young, she wore low-heeled sandals most of the time when "dressing up." After she retired, she wore sneakers pretty much everywhere, even to my brother's wedding, because of painful arthritis in her spine. A fanny pack was her answer to a purse, and for some reason she always left it half open, almost daring someone to steal her wallet. I even bought her a "fancy" leather fanny pack for special occasions.

Her one indulgence when it came to her appearance was manicures, though she never paid for them. She had beautiful hands and was quite adept at painting her nails herself.

Mom drank black coffee all day long, though she let it sit on the table until it was almost cold before drinking it. She also loved a good, thick, medium-rare steak and the occasional hot fudge sundae. She served those sundaes every New Year's Eve, right before midnight, and it became a family tradition I continued with my son. Mom struggled with her weight for most of her life, but after she had a heart attack in her late fifties, she had to give up steak and ice cream, instead subbing in blackberries to satisfy her sweet tooth. When she died, the only thing my brother and I found in her refrigerator was some old cheese, a pint of blackberries, and a can of Reddi Wip.

Mom liked to tell the same slightly risqué jokes, over and over:

"You know how to make a hormone?

"Don't pay 'er."

And then there was this classic:

"You know what really burns my ass?" She would put her hand up at the height of her behind. "A candle about that high."

My mother had a quick wit and a no-nonsense way about her. She had no patience for showing off. Whenever I used what she considered an unnecessarily complicated word—like when I used the word "prestigious" to describe the Wimbledon tennis tournament when I was 10—she would immediately clap back with, "I know a big word, too: delicatessen."

This, too, became something of a tradition, because I hate it when my students try to impress me with fancy vocabulary.

My mother was frank about everything. When I was about six, I asked her where babies came from, and she told me the truth.

"The husband puts his penis in his wife's vagina."

"What if she's not married?"

"Then her boyfriend does it."

For the longest time, I thought this coupling happened right before the baby was born. When the woman wanted a baby, she and her partner went to the hospital, he put his penis in her vagina, and out popped a baby.

Once, when I was about ten, I wanted to cut my Barbie doll's hair. I saw a seam ripper on the shelf in the basement, and I thought that would do the trick. I climbed up on my mom's sewing machine to reach the shelf, but the machine fell and landed on my big toe. I was in terrible pain. I crawled up the stairs to where my mom was vacuuming.

"What's wrong?"

"The (sob) sewing (sob) machine (sob) fell (sob) on my (sob) toe."

"Did you break my sewing machine?"

I ended up in the emergency room. The doctor had to drain the blood from under my toenail, which was black and blue for at least a month and eventually fell off. Yet all my mother seemed to be concerned about, once it was clear that I would live, was the fate of her sewing machine. That was my mom in a nutshell: singularly practical.

She would say the oddest things sometimes, including one story that embarrassed me to no end. The story involved my pediatrician, Dr. Morris Wessel, a pioneering physician who served on the faculty at Yale University. I'm pretty sure she used the story to prove that Dr. Wessel was great at his job, but it never made sense to me.

When I was a baby, she brought me to see Dr. Wessel. As pediatricians do, he asked my mother to remove my onesie and diaper so he could get an accurate weight on me. As he made some notes on his chart, he asked her, "Now, how old is he?"

My mom used to tell this story to my friends when I was an adult. She often recounted it to people the first time she met them. To her, it was a hilarious anecdote about her infant daughter and an eminent physician, but I always felt mortified when she shared it. I was bullied relentlessly when I was a kid because I looked like a boy, and I couldn't figure out why my mom would tell this story, knowing how I was often misgendered, even as an adult. She didn't seem to understand that relating the tale could hurt my feelings. Sometimes, it was as if feelings didn't matter to her. I think maybe it was difficult for her to deal with my feelings because she had trouble with her own emotions. Maybe she was disappointed in how her life turned out. She had her own problems, so helping me deal with mine was probably not high on her priority list.

****

She may have been insensitive, but she was also one of the smartest people I ever knew, and I admired her for that. I think my mother's intelligence scared people. They made fun of her sometimes, but it was partly her own fault. She liked to prove how much she knew, and she would often throw out facts rather than participating in real conversations. She loved to talk about the Defenestration of Prague, which involved people being thrown out of windows long ago. I think the reason she enjoyed bringing it up was because "defenestration" is such an impressive word. (Although she never liked it when other people used these types of words.) Showing off her smarts might have been a coping method; I don't think she had a lot of self-esteem. My friends loved her, though.

"Your mom's so cool," they would say.

I guess it was because she talked to them like real people. She was always joking around and refused to patronize anyone.

"What are you taking up," she'd ask them when they were home from college, "besides time, space and money"?

One of the great achievements of my mother's life was the fact that she appeared on *Jeopardy!* She was on the show in 1968, while she was pregnant with me. She uncovered the Daily Double, but she missed it. She was supposed to name the two planets mentioned in the song "Fly Me to the Moon," but she couldn't. She may not have won, but she got to tell everyone from then on that she'd been on the show, and it always seemed to impress folks. Back then, contestants got to keep the money they earned on the show, even if they didn't win. Of course, people won a lot less back then. I think we got wall-to-wall carpeting with her winnings. She also won a set of encyclopedias, which my brother and I devoured while watching television.

Because I was on the show in utero, it was always a dream of mine to be on *Jeopardy!* as an adult. In 2018, when that finally happened, Alex Trebek mentioned that this was my second appearance.

I was always a trivia buff. I remember acing a test in history class in seventh grade based solely on what I'd learned from following the news, watching TV, and talking to my parents. In my early 30s, I was a bar trivia maven. My friend Julie and I played every week, sometimes twice a week. I don't think we paid for drinks for two years because of all the bar tabs we won. Once, Mom joined us while she was visiting, and of course we came out on top.

But getting on *Jeopardy!* is not as easy as winning bar trivia. The first time I tried out was in the early '90s, when I was still living in Connecticut. My brother and I drove to Atlantic City and spent the day at Merv Griffin's Resorts International casino. I didn't pass the test, but Geoffrey did. He got to go back a few weeks later for an audition. He also won big at the blackjack table after we took the test, and we enjoyed a very nice steak dinner.

I didn't try out again until after I moved to Denver in the early 2000s. By then, the test was online. It's fifty questions with a short timer for each. I must have taken it at least ten times before I got an audition. During my first audition, I was quite nervous and I didn't do very well in the simulated game. A few years and a few online tests later, I got another audition; this time, I was much more comfortable. The first time I rang in, I responded incorrectly, and I must have had a dejected look on my face, because the woman who was in charge encouraged me to keep trying. I did, and I did much better after that with my responses.

A few months later, I received a voicemail from one of the contestant co-ordinators on the show. He said to call him about my audition. When I called back, I spoke with Glenn, another coordinator. He started asking me about my wedding and honeymoon. (During the audition, I told the coordinators that I couldn't tape the show during final exam week or during my honeymoon.) It wasn't until about five minutes into the call that Glenn finally told me I had been selected to appear on the show.

"Think of it as our wedding gift to you," he said.

The trip to LA was amazing. My wife and son came with me, and we spent four nights there. Sunday night we had dinner with my Uncle Donny and his husband, Jon. Monday we biked to the Santa Monica Pier and rode the Ferris wheel. Tuesday, we checked out the La Brea Tar Pits. Wednesday was tape day.

The van picked up all the contestants at the hotel at 7 a.m. They tape five shows a day, so I got to meet about a dozen smart folks who were just as nerdy as me as we all waited for our turn to compete. It was both exciting and nerve-wracking. I kept going to the restroom; I was afraid I was going to have to pee during Final Jeopardy!

Once I got on stage, the whole experience seemed to go by very quickly. I did well, but the category "History of Aviation" was not kind to me. I was in third place going into Final Jeopardy!, so I didn't bet anything and hoped the other contestants bet big and responded incorrectly. The clue had to do with the country closest to of the Isle of Lesbos, and I came up with the correct re-sponse of "What is Turkey?" (The providence of a lesbian getting a clue about Lesbos is not lost on me.) My strategy of not wagering paid off, as the other women guessed wrong, so I would have won even if I didn't answer correctly. I ended up winning $8,800 during that half-hour. And I believe I was the first woman ever to win "Jeopardy!" while wearing a necktie. The only disappoint-ing thing about it was that because I responded correctly in Final Jeopardy!, I could have won a lot more money if I'd wagered.

After my win, I only had about ten minutes until the next show began, and I had to change clothes, so there was no time to savor my victory. But I did get to change in the winner's dressing room, which was amazing. Actually, it's a tiny stall. But who cares. I was a *Jeopardy!* champion!

During the second show, I kicked ass. I had $15,000 after the first two rounds, but I got the Final Jeopardy! response wrong and lost by a dollar. (Oh, how I wish I had read *Treasure Island* when I was young. Damn you, Robert Louis Stevenson!) I was so nervous that I didn't read the clue carefully and then panicked. I didn't feel that bad about losing, though, because I probably wouldn't have gotten the correct response even if I'd read the clue correctly. And despite blowing my big lead in game two, I was very happy when I left Sony Studios. The experience was one of the best days of my life. And the money wasn't bad, either. After coming in second on day two, I got another 2,000 bucks, for a total of $10,800. Not a huge payday by any measure, but still not bad for an hour of work.

It's cool when you think about all the people who try out for "Jeopardy!" Approximately 100,000 folks take the online test every year, about 3,000 get an audition, and a few hundred make it onto the show. To be one of the lucky ones to earn a place on the show is an amazing achievement that I am extremely proud of. To actually win a game was icing on the cake.

I think the best thing to come out of my appearance on *Jeopardy!* was the friendships I've made with other contestants through Facebook. It's an amazing group of people who share their joys, their sorrows, and their fears.

Now, when people find out that I was on the show, they want to know all about it. I am finally cool for being a nerd.

***

I was born in September 1968 in New Haven, Connecticut. I came into the world after Martin Luther King Jr. and Bobby Kennedy were assassinated but before Richard Nixon was elected president. For some reason that fact has always seemed important to me. King is still one of my heroes. The turmoil of that long ago summer percolates in my mind, informing my thoughts about what it means to be an American, and what it means to be a white, liberal Jew. As a young adult, I often wished I had been in high school or college during 1968. I like to think I would have been a radical, out in the streets marching for change. Watching and listening to the political and personal choices my mother made inspired me to take a similar approach. I wonder if I have done her proud in that regard.

***

I was named Lynn Michelle for my maternal grandfather, Michael Lee. Mom always told me she had wanted a boy first, and then a girl; she got her wish, though not as quickly as she'd hoped. Mom and Dad were eager to have another child after Geoffrey was born, but my mom couldn't get pregnant until she had an operation on her cervix. She cried tears of joy when the doctor told her I was a girl. I guess she really wanted me.

I was born before natural childbirth was in fashion, but my mother wasn't administered any drugs during labor. This wasn't done deliberately. She kept telling the nurses she thought it was time for the baby to come, but they told her to be patient. She and the nurses were doing the *New York Times* Sunday crossword puzzle together. (Is it any wonder I make it a point to try to finish the *Times* crossword every day?) My mother was as patient as she could be, but it was too late for an epidural by the time the nurses realized she was right.

When I was a few months old, Grandma Clara noticed that I crawled funny. It turned out that I had been born with a broken hip. An operation fixed the problem, but I had to wear a body cast for the next year or so. I still managed to crawl, though. My parents would drag me around on a board with wheels–a cheap version of a little red wagon.

Our parents loved us very much, but they also put the fear of God into Geoffrey and me. I spent much of my childhood simply being too afraid to misbehave. If I ever acted in any way that wasn't perfect, Dad would yell or Mom would threaten me.

"Do you want to be embarrassed right here, in front of all these people?" she'd say. We might be in the supermarket, at the mall, or at a party. I didn't know if it was going to be a sharp smack or a loud reprimand, but I learned never to misbehave in front of her.

Mom used to brag about this threat to everyone who would listen. She seemed to think she possessed a great parenting secret. I didn't realize until I was grown up how much damage it did to me. I was literally scared to death of my mother. To this day, I fear confrontation of any kind. My mood changes when I feel someone I care about is angry with me; this has caused a lot of friction between me and my romantic partners over the years.

My brother wasn't immune to mom's temper.

Another incident she used to brag about occurred when Geoffrey refused to get ready to go out. He was reading the *Guinness Book of World Records*. She kept telling him it was time to go, and he just kept reading. She got angrier and angrier. Finally, she took the book from him and ripped it to shreds as he watched.

My mother often joked about this encounter, and when I was young, I laughed along with her. But once I became a parent myself, I realized how traumatizing it must have been for Geoffrey. Mom was never physically abusive, but her words and actions often cut to the bone.

Unfortunately, that was something I learned from my mom, too. When my son was very young, I would yell a lot. When I was getting him ready for preschool, if he didn't want to go out the door, I'd scream at him. I didn't seem to realize that he was just a little boy who needed someone to soothe him, not frighten him. Sometimes I'd kick the refrigerator when I got mad.

But eventually, I thought about the way my mother invoked fear in my heart, and I resolved to work hard to make sure my son wasn't afraid of me. Since I began a Twelve-Step program about ten years ago, I haven't yelled at him like this or kicked anything. Sure, I get mad sometimes, and I even swear occasionally, but it's nothing like what I used to do. I take after my mother in a lot of ways, but I stopped putting the fear of God into my son when he was very young. For that, I'm truly proud of myself. Not all traditions need to be passed on.

***

Mom certainly wasn't perfect, but she had a lot of good qualities, too.

When she met a woman who wanted to leave her abusive partner, she invited the woman to stay with us for a few weeks until she got on her feet.

She refused to buy grapes for years in solidarity with the United Farm Workers.

She taught me about racial injustice.

And she encouraged me to write.

Writing was the first thing I was really good at, other than sports. I remember when we learned how to diagram sentences in sixth grade. I was one of only a few students in the class who enjoyed it. When I got to high school, I learned how to write a research paper. My freshman English teacher, Miss Coppini, had us write about the news events that occurred around the day we were born. We used microfilm from *The New York Times* to conduct research. I had the time of my life.

One of the first assignments Miss Coppini had us do was to write a paragraph about what we saw out the window. I wrote about a tree with one leaf desperately clinging to it. My teacher loved it. So did Mom.

"You should be a reporter," my mom told me. That rare moment of praise stayed with me.

I had always loved reading the newspaper, so her advice made sense. While other kids were reading actual books, I was devouring the local papers and even *The New York Times*. I watched 60 Minutes with Mom and Dad every week. I wrote for my high school paper and so impressed my teacher that she assigned me the school's monthly column in *The New Haven Register*, the large metro daily in our region. My most controversial piece was about the school's cafeteria offerings. I got dirty looks from the kitchen staff for a month afterward. From that point on, I had to approve all columns with my teacher before sending them in. I became a copy editor and eventually earned my Ph.D. in journalism. Today I am a journalism professor, a job that I truly love.

***

I also got my love of Judaism from my mom. She used to tell me that when she was a girl, she would accompany her father to synagogue on Saturdays. Her older sister made fun of her for this. No one else in the family bothered to go. When Mom and Dad first took me to services, I was bored. But I learned to love the ritual, the singing, and the community that it brought into my life. My favorite holiday has always been Passover, the celebration of the Israelites' flight from slavery to freedom.

My family used to host huge Seders each year. The Seder is the feast held on the first and second nights of the holiday. I say my family hosted these, but it was really my mother who served as host. It always seemed like she spent the month before Passover preparing. She made a huge pot of chicken soup, which she would freeze until the Seder, and brisket with carrots and onions. She even made her own chopped liver, which was to die for. For dessert, she made a special angel food cake with no flour and many, many eggs, which she had to store upside down for hours so it wouldn't fall in. Then she added fresh strawberries and homemade whipped cream to make kosher-for-Passover strawberry shortcake. But the *piece de resistance* was always her latkes—potato pancakes. She made the best latkes I've ever tasted. Most families only have latkes once a year, on Hanukkah, but my mom's were so good that she made them for all the big Jewish holidays, including Passover and Rosh Hashanah. We would top them with apple sauce and sour cream.

Although we didn't eat bread on Passover, we did not keep kosher in other ways, so my mom had no problem serving sour cream with brisket. (If you keep kosher, you're not supposed to have milk products with meat because the Bible says not to "cook a kid in its mother's milk." But the prohibition includes chicken for some reason, which makes it a silly rule because chickens don't give milk to their chicks, so I don't mind ignoring this and other Kosher laws.) Once, when my grandmother's brother was at the Seder, I asked my mom why she hadn't put the sour cream on the table. My great uncle yelled at me.

"You can't have sour cream with brisket!"

"Why not?" I wanted to know.

I literally had no idea.

We may have had no problem eating sour cream with brisket, even on Passover, but my family went all out in other ways. Even though the Bible only bans five specific grains on the holiday (wheat, oats, barley, rye, and spelt), the Eastern European Rabbis came up with all kinds of additional rules. Legumes and corn were not allowed for some odd reason, so we couldn't have peanut butter. My mother, however, had no qualms about frying her latkes in peanut oil. She always said it was allowed, but I am not so sure. The ban on corn meant there were a lot of things we couldn't indulge in over the holiday, like most of the soda on the shelf at the grocery stores, which contained corn syrup. We didn't drink much soda in my house, but my parents allowed it on special occasions. My mom bought something called "Cott" soda, which was the only one made with real sugar back then. And although Easter always fell around Passover, we couldn't have any Easter candy because it usually contained corn syrup as well. We had to have candy that was specifically made "kosher for Passover." It tasted good, for sure, but it was also a reminder that, as a Jew, I was different from most of the people around me. I was one of the few Jews in my school, and I had very few Jewish friends growing up.

I remember once when I was in grammar school, my mom made me a thermos full of matzo ball soup for lunch. It was one of my favorite meals, and I was so excited to have it. Then one of my friends asked me what it was, and I told her.

"Lynn's having moth ball soup," she told everyone within shouting distance.

My excitement turned to a pit in the bottom of my stomach, and I was no longer hungry. I guess when it came down to it, making fun of someone for a cheap laugh was easier than trying to understand a different culture.

But in another way, it made me feel special to have to follow a strict set of rules about what I put in my body for one week of the year. I continued to follow that ultra-strict diet until just a few years ago, when the Conservative Rabbis announced that it was okay to eat corn and legumes on Passover. So now I can have Easter candy, though I still buy soda with pure cane sugar. I also avoid wheat, oats, barley, rye or spelt during Passover. (I'm not sure I've ever eaten spelt.) And I endure matzo for seven days a year. I say "endure" because matzo — also known as "the bread of affliction" — has little resemblance to matzo ball soup and does a number on my digestive tract, but some things are too important to give up.

I still make my mom's latkes three times a year, just like she did. They are my son's favorite food. And I still serve sour cream with the brisket. I have yet to attempt her strawberry shortcake recipe.

Did I mention that my mom shopped and cooked for her Passover feast while working full time? It's ironic that Passover is about freedom, but my mom was usually in the kitchen most of the night during the Seder. My father served as leader, sitting at the head of the table and directing who would read at certain points. But I always saw it as my mom's Seder. My parents might have been very liberal in some ways, but when it came to cooking and Seder, they were traditional.

I try to have a Seder every year—not as big as my mom's—but I always invite a few friends. I love hosting people who've never been to a Seder before. It brings me joy to share my traditions with my non-Jewish friends.

The rituals and traditions of Judaism bring me closer to my ancestors. I feel a kinship with those who came before because they said some of the same prayers I say today. I didn't know three of my grandparents, but living a Jewish life means I have something very powerful in common with them. Belonging to a synagogue also makes me part of a community, and knowing that I am passing these traditions down to my son is important, too. I don't think he appreciates religion right now, but at least he knows where he came from. Perhaps someday he'll treasure it as much as I do.

I'm one of those people who sing loudly and off-key during services. I'm sure I embarrass my family, but the prayers and songs bring me such joy that it's difficult to hold back. Sometimes I even sway back and forth while I pray; I get caught up in it and it just feels natural. I know some Orthodox Jews do this when they pray, too. It's another way I feel connected to my heritage.

While I was in college, I was very involved in Hillel, the Jewish student organization. I attended services, retreats, and social events regularly; it was a way of bringing home to a faraway place. I took Hebrew classes for two years, and while I never really grasped the language, I got to know a lot of Jewish students, one of whom became my best college friend. One of these Jewish students introduced me to the music of Debbie Friedman, a cantor and folk singer. I became an avid fan. I think my love of her music brought me closer to God. Those songs I fell in love with at 21 still make me feel close to the divine.

During graduation weekend, I took Mom and Dad to Hillel to show them around and introduce them to the rabbi. On the way back to my apartment, I told them I might want to study religion in graduate school.

"You could be a rabbi," Mom said, pride in her voice.

Me? Lead a congregation? Did my mother really think I could fill such an important role? I was honored but shocked. I had never thought about doing anything of the sort.

What I really wanted to do was get my master's or Ph.D. in religious studies. But for a long time, I looked up to my mother so much that I did pretty much anything she advised. So, I decided right then and there that I would apply to rabbinical school. I had never taught Sunday school or anything like that, so in my application essay I focused on my love of my home synagogue. The admissions committee told me to become more involved and reapply. It seemed like too much trouble, and I was ashamed for not getting in, so I gave up on the idea of becoming a rabbi. It's probably a good thing I didn't get in. I don't think I would have liked being a rabbi. I'm not really a "people" person.

I may have given up on rabbinical school, but I never gave up on Judaism. I have pretty much always belonged to a synagogue. Many people wait until they have children old enough for religious school before joining, but not me. I try my best to attend services regularly. Of course I attend on the High Holidays, and I used to blow the shofar (ram's horn) at the end of Yom Kippur, the holiest day of the year. Sometimes when I look at our rabbi delivering a sermon or leading a Passover seder, I feel a pang of envy. But I realize that my life is the way it's supposed to be. I love Judaism, and I enjoy my synagogue, and I believe in God profoundly. It's an important part of my life. If it weren't for my reliance on God, I don't think I would be where I am today. But I wasn't meant to be a rabbi. I was meant to teach people how to write. It's what I'm best at. It's what I love. And it's quite fulfilling.

***

Of course, being Jewish meant being different. I remember my mother telling me many times, with pain in her voice, that she was forced to say the Lord's Prayer every morning of her public-school education in Buffalo. (Many people don't realize that the *Our Father* is a Christian prayer, but it is.) I could tell that my mom was deeply affected by this daily dose of discrimination. Although I didn't deal with discrimination on a regular basis, I did face a few incidents of antisemitism growing up, and I remember them vividly.

The most hurtful of these occurred when I was in high school. During my senior year, I was the captain of the soccer team and the starting goalkeeper. The day before Yom Kippur — a day when Jews are supposed to fast and refrain from all work — the coach announced that we had practice the next day, even though there was no school. I told him I wouldn't be there because of the holiday. He said it didn't matter, the practice was mandatory, and if I skipped it, I wouldn't be able to play in the next game. All the other girls on the team protested. "Lynn's Jewish. She can't come to practice on Yom Kippur." But that didn't change the coach's mind.

When I got home, I told my mother, who was livid. She immediately called the school's athletic director, Miss Fraser, who was also the softball coach and knew my family well. Miss Fraser agreed that the coach had erred and said she would talk to him about the issue.

I did not start the next game, but I did play in the second half. Nevertheless, I did not play goalie again during my high school career. Instead, I was moved to forward, which was not my best position. I don't know if the coach was just waiting to replace me as the goalie or if this was payback for missing practice, or both. He never discussed the move with me, which made it even worse.

Around that same time, the manager at my after-school job at Burger King stopped scheduling me after I took the High Holidays off.

Those weren't not the only antisemitic incidents I endured as a young person.

When I was in grammar school, a boy threw a penny on the floor and told me to chase it, using the word "Jew" as a slur.

Then there was the time when I was in my first year at Indiana and someone tried to sell me a ticket to the Sting concert during dinner. I asked how much he wanted, but the price seemed too high. My roommate asked me, "Why didn't you Jew him down"? I was appalled. I knew that some people used that phrase, but I'd never heard it personally. I let her have it and walked out. She came up to the room a few minutes later and seemed extremely sorry. She said she honestly hadn't known that the expression was discriminatory. She was from a small town in Indiana, and I doubt she even knew what antisemitism was.

In a women's studies class in graduate school, I brought up the idea that using BC and AD with dates was Christian-centric and to be avoided. BC stands for "Before Christ" and AD stands for "Anno Domini," which is Latin for "in the year of our Lord." I explained that BCE and CE, which stand for "Before the Common Era" and "Common Era," are more inclusive. I wondered aloud why the Jewish scholar who wrote the chapter we were discussing would use BC and AD. The professor said we had to move on. When I asked her about the issue after class, she told me my question was "trite." The ironic thing was that this professor spent a lot of time discussing the discrimination faced by women of color, but when I brought up how Jewish women might be offended by something, I was shot down. I was angry and almost complained to the department chair, but I thought better of it. Sometimes I still regret that decision.

Perhaps these incidents are part of the reason why I take so much pride in my Jewish heritage. Why I always make a big dinner on the eve of Rosh Hashanah. Why I fast on Yom Kippur. Why I always take the High Holidays off from work. (And since the Burger King incident, none of my supervisors have ever complained.)

These occurrences also might play a role in why I am so disgusted by discrimination of any kind, and why I have always fought for justice for the oppressed. Whether it's women, LGBTQ+ folks, Jews, Muslims, Blacks or any other marginalized group, I can't stand to see people made to suffer for who they are.

***

My mother also had a profound influence on my choice to study at Indiana University.

I knew I wanted to leave the Northeast and study journalism at a big school. My mom was a guidance counselor, so she helped me figure out which colleges had the best J-schools. At the time, my best options were Indiana, Northwestern, Wisconsin, and North Carolina.

Frankly, I didn't think I'd get into Northwestern. I was ranked in the top 20 of my graduating class of about 200, but I never thought of myself as a great student. I hardly ever studied. I did very well in subjects for which I could write, such as English and history, but when it came to classes like math, science, and language, where it didn't come easily, I just gave up. I dropped my honors science and math courses before senior year. I never took physics because I was afraid it would be too difficult. This idea of not trying things that were hard followed me for a long time.

But even though I didn't think of myself as a great student, I applied to Northwestern anyway. I wrote the essays and endured the interview.

My first choice was North Carolina, but I didn't get in. It is a notoriously difficult school for out-of-state students to gain entrance. Indiana and Wisconsin were no problem getting into as an honors student with a pretty good GPA.

I had a great time on my visit to Indiana. I flew to Indianapolis by myself and rode a limo to Bloomington. I'm not sure why limousines transported students to and from the airport back then, but it sure was fun. It rained the day of the campus tour, but I loved it anyway: a large campus with a beautiful arboretum, and the limestone buildings impressed me. It didn't hurt that the men's basketball team had won four NCAA titles and was about to win its fifth.

Then I got my acceptance letter from Northwestern. I was stunned. The large envelope contained a smaller envelope that looked like it had been damaged en route and sent back to campus, which explained why I had gotten my letter so late. But my mother had another explanation.

"You were probably the last person they admitted," she said, laughing. She thought this was so funny that she insisted on telling anyone who'd listen.

I was hurt by her remark, but I was so afraid of my parents that I didn't say anything. I internalized the hurt and figured she was probably right. For many years after that, I continued to think that I wasn't good enough.

She also told me we didn't have the money for Northwestern, although my father said we could figure out a way for me to attend. Northwestern was more than double the cost of Indiana was for out-of-state students, so if I went to Bloomington, I could graduate without student loans. And I know it was the right decision. I was challenged there. The journalism school was one of the best in the country, and I flourished at the student newspaper. I was involved in extra-curricular activities and made a lot of lifelong friends. But part of me still wonders what it would have been like to attend a more elite school.

Looking back, perhaps my mother's comment about me being the last person admitted was a way to deflect from the fact that she felt bad about not having the money. Or maybe she was jealous that I had gotten into a top school, while she had attended a local college.

Whatever the case, she clung to it as a way to hurt me for a long time. Years later, she used to tell me over and over that "If you'd gone to Northwestern, we never would have gotten divorced." My parents split up about a year after I graduated from college, and she thought she wouldn't have had the money to make it on her own if she and my dad had had to pay for a private school. Then again, it was my dad who left her, not the other way around, so I'm not sure how Northwestern would have been relevant.

The funny thing about my mom's comment linking the divorce and Northwestern is that my dad wanted nothing to do with the house once he left. My mom got all the money when she sold it after living there for thirty years. I admit that Northwestern was much pricier than Indiana, but it always felt like she was blaming me.

I also know now that part of the reason I didn't go to Northwestern was because I didn't push back and demand to go. I feel like I could have persuaded her, with my dad's help, if I'd really tried. Yes, I possessed a very real fear of my mother, but I also nursed a very deep fear of failure. I've always been a bit of a selective perfectionist. If I'm good at something, I work at it until I'm the best I can be. But if something doesn't come easily, I give up. In college, if a reading was too hard, instead of rereading it, I'd just put it away. When Hebrew became too difficult for me to master with minimal studying, I gave up and took the C. I hardly tried in my geology and biology classes because the material simply didn't come naturally. I wish now that I had put in the effort to learn when things got tough.

This fear of failure became a method of self-sabotage throughout my life. I was one of the most talented journalists at the campus paper at Indiana, and everyone assumed I would apply to be editor-in-chief during my final semester. But I didn't do it because I feared I wouldn't be good enough. I have always regretted that decision.

For a long time, I resented people who attended private schools, simply because I "wasn't allowed" to attend Northwestern. Even now, when I meet people who attended the school, I feel a bit of envy. I was jealous because I thought I could've done better for myself if I'd been a Northwestern grad. I could have gotten better jobs, earned more money, maybe gone to law school (always my secret dream.) Most of all, I could have proved to people that I was the smartest person in the room. And I resented my mother for not letting me go there.

But I see now that it wasn't all her fault. I see that I didn't have the confidence in myself to push to go there. I was so full of fear that I couldn't think straight. But I know that Indiana was the perfect place for me to incubate my writing and editing talent, as well as to become a better human being. I loved my time in Bloomington, and I wouldn't exchange it for anything.

One of the best things I did at IU was join the co-ed service fraternity Alpha Phi Omega. We helped run blood drives and drove women safely around campus, and when I was a senior, I spearheaded a canned food drive. I served as newsletter editor and vice president of communications for the group.

My time in Alpha Phi Omega also led me to one of my first acts of rebellion. The fraternity always ended events with what we called our "toast song." The last lines went like this: "Come and join in song together. Brothers all are we. Daily working, daily striving evermore to be, men of Alpha Phi Omega, our fraternity." It made sense that the song originally referred to men because the group was all-male when it was founded in 1925. Nevertheless, when I joined in the late 1980s, there were more women than men in my chapter. A couple of us wanted to change the song to make it more inclusive. I spoke about the issue in front of our chapter and again at the state convention. I remember one woman coming up to me after my convention speech. She raised an eyebrow and pursed her lips: "Are you gonna change the Bible next?"

I was taken aback, to say the least. I couldn't see how a woman could be so against a change that would make her organization more inclusive to people like her. A year or so later, the movement to change the song got as far as the national convention, which I did not attend. Our chapter's two representatives weren't sure how the chapter would want them to vote, so they split their votes. The movement failed.

I didn't realize it at the time, but my failed efforts to change the toast song were reminiscent of my mother's work in the women's movement. I saw an injustice and worked to change it for the better. I not only have my mother to thank for leading me down the path to Indiana and Alpha Phi Omega, but once I got there, I followed in her footsteps. And the organization did, finally, change the song a few years later.

Another positive thing my mom did for me was to help me secure an internship at the Bridgeport Post (now the Connecticut Post) after my junior year at Indiana. I had applied to several newspapers in Connecticut—as well as a few bigtime papers outside my home state—and I got an interview with the editorial page editor at the Post. He offered me the internship, and I was excited. But a week before the gig was about to start, he called to say that because of budget considerations, the paper was cancelling all its summer internships. I knew I needed an internship at a large daily paper to get a good job when I graduated, so this was devastating. I called my mother to tell her what had happened, and fearing what she might do, I practically begged her not to call the editor to complain. ... She didn't call the editor.

She called the PUBLISHER.

I couldn't be mad at her for long, though, because whatever she told him worked, and I was one of only two interns hired that summer. It worked out well for me, because I eventually landed a job at the very same paper when I graduated a year later. I started as an emergency substitute, but the editors liked me so much that I was hired full-time. I worked as a copy editor for about four years before starting graduate school. I deserved the job, and I deserved the internship, but my mother's assertiveness—possibly an outgrowth of the confidence she gained in her work in the women's movement—helped me get my start at the newspaper.

My mother had her warts, and they certainly showed, but doesn't everyone? Perhaps I loved her because she was so human. She was much more than a parent. In many ways, she was also a friend. I remember Mom taking me to New York City each summer when I was young. We'd ride the train into Grand Central Station and get coffee and a snack at a diner. (This was years before places like Starbucks took over the coffee shop industry.) Then we'd take the subway to Times Square and stand in line for half-price tickets to see a Broadway show. We saw a few Neil Simon plays; one year we caught *A Chorus Line*, and we saw *Driving Miss Daisy* when it was off-Broadway. We'd go to lunch before the show, and sometimes we'd meet my dad for dinner afterward.

I remember once we were in line for tickets and my mom gave me some money to get an Orange Julius. I must have been about 12. Back home in Milford, you could cross the street diagonally downtown, so that's what I did. I was feeling quite proud of myself, drinking my Orange Julius, smiling and waving to my mom. She had the oddest look on her face. I didn't realize until later that I had literally taken my life into my hands. Luckily, I made it across the busy intersection in one piece. Despite my near-death experience, these trips brought us closer together, and attending Broadway shows made me feel grown up.

She was not a traditional mother by any means, but she sure could bake. Mom was known for her amazing fruit pies. She made apple, blueberry, and strawberry-rhubarb. The crusts were the best part. She always said her secret was Crisco. We had an old dishwasher that we'd wheel over to the sink to use, and I'd help her roll the crust out on the top of it. I used to get yelled at for eating raw pie crust. I couldn't help it; it was delicious. Sometimes, when there were leftovers, I would sneak bits of the crust off the edge of the pie when I walked by. I have made many pies in my life, but none as good as my mom's.

She also got me to help her with the chores, sometimes in amusing ways. When she took the laundry down to the basement, she would tell me to follow her, then she'd drop several items of clothing on the stairs. When I got older, I realized she dropped the clothes on purpose, so I would feel needed.

She had a wicked sense of humor. She could make anything funny. Sometimes she would imitate me, copying everything I said and mimicking my gestures. At first, I would get upset, but then we would both start laughing hysterically.

I spent a lot of time being embarrassed by my mother and father when I was a teenager. To put it bluntly, they were nerds. My father used to wear plaid pants with a striped shirt, and my mother wrote sweats outside the house long before it was cool.

One of my favorite places to eat was Burger King, but if my parents suggested going there, I'd tell them to go through the drive thru. I didn't want to be seen with them.

When I became an adult, that all changed. It became a pleasure to hang out with Mom. We once took a bus trip to Washington, D.C., and had a blast wandering the museums and eating at fancy restaurants. When I was a doctoral student at Ohio University, I spent one summer at Mom's condo in North Carolina. It was fun just being with her.

She was a lifelong Democrat, just like me. When I moved to Colorado, we'd often have several short telephone conversations throughout the day, just chatting about what we'd seen in the news. She was addicted to C-SPAN and MSNBC. I didn't have TV for years, but when I finally got one, I started watching MSNBC, too, so I could continue those conversations with Mom.

Another thing we had in common was a love of education. She had a master's and a sixth-year degree, which is training beyond a master's. I think this was one of the reasons I decided to go to graduate school; I'd seen it modeled for me, and I believed it was an important credential.

It wasn't until I was a doctoral student that I realized how smart I was, though. I was very successful as a Ph.D. student. I finished all my doctoral work in three years, including writing my dissertation. Many people take longer, and some never finish.

My research focused on the relationship between one WNBA team and its hometown newspaper. It wasn't the greatest dissertation ever written, by far, but it taught me that I could push myself and do things I never thought I could do. I was voted the top Ph.D. student in the journalism program my last year at Ohio University. I had finally finished something that didn't come easily.

I remember visiting Mom every year in December, during my break from teaching. We wouldn't do anything special; sometimes we'd go out to eat or take in a University of North Carolina women's basketball game. That was another thing we had in common: a love of women's basketball. After I fell in love with the sport and started researching it, she got hooked, too. For several years we attended the Women's Regional NCAA basketball tournament together. We went to Richmond, Hartford, Dayton, and Denver. It was a thrill each time. But most of the time we'd just sit around watching the news or one of the many iterations of *Law and Order*. (We both loved that show.) It was so easy to be with her.

Although she only had a few friends, she was loyal to them. One of her best friends was Fran, our neighbor growing up. She was an Irish Catholic with a rather conservative bent, while Mom was a Jewish liberal. But they were besties for a long time. Some of my favorite memories involve sitting in Fran's kitchen, or Beverly's or Lois's, and drinking tea while Mom and her friends shared their hopes, their dreams, their sorrows, and their strengths.

Gloria Steinem said it perfectly in her book, *My Life on the Road*: "[T]he women's movement was born of women talking to each other." [1]

But maybe I needed to talk more deeply with my mom. I should have asked her about her life. She often hinted that it was disappointing, but I was too embarrassed to acknowledge her suffering and inquire. And because of how she treated me as a child, I was sometimes afraid of her emotionally.

To make it worse, she often acted in ways that seemed inappropriate to me.

I remember being at parties with her several times when I was teen and hearing her joke loudly about sex, which deeply embarrassed me. When I complained, she called me a prude. She also talked negatively about my father in front of me after they divorced. Even though I was an adult when this happened, I felt hurt.

I think she told me what she really felt about my dad because she saw me as a confidant rather than as her child.

One thing I never asked her about was a comment that concerns me to this day: "Men rape their wives."

---

1. Steinem, G. (2015) *My Life on the Road*, Random House, New York. Page 115.

She only said it once that I remember, but a statement like that is difficult to forget. Was she just speaking in general terms? Had she heard this from a friend? Was she talking about her own experience?

The fact that my mother even brought up this subject is hard for me to think about, but, in a way, it encapsulates our relationship. Once I grew up, my mom and I became more than mother and daughter; we became best friends. "Men rape their wives" is really something a woman tells her best friend, not her child.

Another thing I never asked about was something Grandma Clara mentioned once about her honeymoon.

"I came back the same way I left."

I never questioned Grandma about this statement, but I assume it meant she didn't have sex. I wonder if she even knew about sex before her wedding night. She was born in 1905. Did parents tell their kids about the birds and the bees back then? Maybe she found out just before she walked down the aisle. What a shock that would have been. Perhaps they tried to have sex, and it was too painful for my grandmother. Maybe my grandfather wasn't very adept. Maybe he was clumsy. Maybe he was rough. Or maybe she just wasn't in the mood, and my grandfather acted like a gentleman and went to sleep.

Although sex can be a difficult subject for parents and children to discuss, I think it's important. My son is becoming a man, and I want him to treat his future partners with respect. It's also important to me because, simply put, women are people, and they have a right to say "no" to sex at any time. They should have dominion over their bodies. They should be able to make their own choices when it comes to medical decisions. They have a right to lead the kind of lives they build for themselves rather than having to conform to external expectations.

Because of the hard work of feminists like my mother, I had opportunities she and my grandmother never had. I was expected to go to college, to make a career for myself. I was never pressured to date or get married. I was never yelled at for being a tomboy. When I came out as queer, I was embraced by my family.

***

All of these thoughts were racing through my head as I boarded the flight to North Carolina.

"It's just a cold," she had said when I called her a few days earlier. "Don't come. I'll need help after I get home. You can come then."

I believed her. And one last time, I didn't question her authority.

Two days later, the doctor called. "You'd better come."

So once again I made a last-minute reservation and prepared to fly to North Carolina. This time I packed a suit.

Just before I left for the airport, I called the hospital and asked the nurse to put the phone up to my mom's ear.

"I love you," I said.

"I love you very much," she answered. I could hear the tears. It was the last time I would hear her voice.

And as the plane lifted off, I prayed:

"God, let her live until I get there. And please don't let her suffer."

Both wishes came true. I arrived at the hospital at about 3 p.m. She was already unconscious but still breathing. The nurse had given her morphine, so she wasn't suffering. I spent the next two hours sitting by her side, holding her hand, and praying. At 5 p.m., after consultation with the doctor, Geoffrey and I agreed to turn off the machine that was helping her breathe. Over the next 15 minutes, her breathing became more labored.

We both held her hands for the last couple of minutes. When the machine flatlined, we each kissed her forehead. Then the strangest thing happened. She began breathing again for about a minute. Then she was gone. That last moment gave me hope that maybe, just maybe, she knew I was there.

For months after her death, I beat myself up for not flying out to be with her as soon as I heard she was in the hospital. I should have known that those were her last days. I could have talked to her and told her how much she meant to me.

"Whatever happened was supposed to happen," Geoffrey said.

He's right, of course. I think Mom didn't want us to see her suffering. Maybe that's why she didn't want us to be there when she was on the ventilator. She told me a few times over the years that neither of her parents needed bedpans when they were dying; she seemed to think using them was some sort of failure. They maintained their dignity until the end, and so did she.

✳✳✳

I miss Mom very much. But when I think of her, I don't mourn her as much as celebrate her. It has only been in the years since she died that I have come to recognize her faults, which could be profound. She was a loving woman who sometimes treated me terribly. But when I think about how lucky I was to spend 45 years with this amazing woman, I can't help but smile.

I grew up near the beach, but I was never a beach person. I didn't realize how important it was to me until I moved away. Now, when I return to my hometown, I always drive to the shore, open the window and drink in the smell of the ocean. It's the smell of my childhood. The smell of home.

It's the same with the mountains. I'm afraid of heights, so I don't ski, and the idea of driving through the mountains to get somewhere interesting scares me. Yet when I walk near my condo in Colorado, I get a spectacular view of the Flatirons outside Boulder and the snow-capped peaks beyond. I often say "*Hallelujah*," which translates to "praise God" in Hebrew, to myself when I see the mountains in all their majesty like this.

When I think about my attitude toward the beach and the mountains, I understand that things aren't black and white. You can appreciate the shoreline even though you're not a "beach person." You can love the mountains even though you fear them. I guess it's the same with parents. You can love someone although she sometimes treated you badly. You can call your mother your best friend, even though you were deathly afraid of her when you were young.

***

When I was in graduate school, I spent most of my time researching and writing about the press and women's basketball, so it made sense to minor in women's studies. After learning so much about women's history and feminist theory, and after seeing how female athletes had been treated throughout the years, I decided I had to do something. I legally changed my last name from Silverstein (my father's name) to include my mother's name: Klyde-Silverstein. (I eventually dropped Silverstein altogether. It was nothing against my father. I just didn't like being hyphenated.) I told everyone I added my mom's name to honor her family, which to me seemed just as important as my father's family. But looking back now, I think I did it to honor my mother and all she did for me. She lost her name when she was just a child. She gave up her name when she got married, although she took back her last name a few years after the divorce.

She gave me life. She helped me get to where I am today. The least I could do is honor her with my name. A feminist act in honor of the ultimate feminist.

Now it's my turn to be a parent. I am trying to raise a caring, feminist boy who isn't afraid of his emotions. And I am trying to make sure that my son is not afraid of me. It's not easy. When it gets tough, I think of Mom and all she went through. And I know that if I'm half the person she was, I can do anything.

When I think of my mother, I sometimes think of Helen Reddy's feminist anthem, and I want to change the lyrics just a bit, to honor my mother: "She is woman; hear her roar."

When I hear the song's chorus, I remember how much I got from my mom, and from feminism, and I really do believe that I am strong … and invincible.

My brother and me when I was quite young. He's six years older than I am.

The day before my brother's Bar Mitzvah in 1975.

Looks like my third birthday. Somehow, they got me to wear a dress.

3

Take me out to the ballgame

Some girls play with dolls. I played with baseball cards. I had a big box full of them, and I used them to play elaborate all-star games. I'd sit in my room and take out my cards. Picking out my favorite players, I'd divide the cards into two teams; one team would play defense while the other was up at bat. One at a time, the players would step into the batter's box. I'd throw a small rock toward each card, and the card would "hit" the rock and run around the bases. My favorite players got the best hits.

I don't think Pete Rose ever made an out during these baseball love fests. I relished the way he played the game. Always hustling. Always giving his all. When I played, I used to run to first base when I earned a walk, just to emulate him. I played first base, just like him, and when I would make the final out of an inning, I'd throw the ball down on the bag, just like my idol.

Baseball was my first love. When I was seven, I proudly wore a blue and red jacket with the logos of every Major League team.

When I was eight, it was time to join a real team. I was one of only a few girls at the tryout. This was 1976, and not many girls were playing organized sports back then. In fact, a New Jersey girl named Maria Pepe had sued Little League in 1972 after being thrown off the team because "girls are not eligible." She won her case, so Little League had to start accepting girls. Still, Little League did not accept all children who wanted to play. Kids who weren't that good didn't make the team. I played in the Milford Junior-Major League, which accepted all comers. There were tryouts, but I think those were used to make sure the teams were well-balanced.

Some of the boys made a big deal out of my being at the tryout. Whispers of "There's a girl here" spread through the sea of wannabe players. I bet they were surprised when I actually caught the balls the coaches threw my way.

Back then, the defensive players used to yell "Let's go, let's go, he's not batter" to try to psyche out the hitters. When I came up, someone would always shout, "It's a girl, move in." More than once, I promptly hit the ball over the infielders' heads.

I played organized baseball until I was 13, and I turned into one of the better players on my team. In my very last game, I drove in six runs. In my final at-bat, I hit a grand slam. My teammates were impressed, and the coaches awarded me the game ball. There's no better feeling in the world than running around the bases after belting the ball over the fence.

But sometimes I felt different. My teammates accepted me with no problems that I was aware of; I guess I was the one who didn't accept myself. If I had been a boy, I would have fit right in on the field. But I wasn't.

***

I used to sit in the basement every weekend when I was a kid, watching the game on TV. I knew all the players' names, numbers, and positions. My father would come in, all sweaty from mowing the lawn.

"Wanna play catch?" he would ask.

"Sure," I'd say.

It was the same every week. We would put on our cleats and grab our gloves and caps. Then we would throw the ball back and forth for about a half hour. He would give me a few grounders and always ended with a pop-up. This scene was repeated a few hundred times between the time I was eight and the time I turned eighteen. These were the best times I ever had with my dad. He wasn't a man of many words, but he said a lot through baseball. It was his way of showing he loved me, that he cared about me. He taught me to love the game—the way to play the *right* way. To win with grace and lose with dignity.

My dad and I bonded through sports. We'd watch football all day long on Sundays during fall and winter, and baseball all summer. I was lucky. My brother was never a sports fan. I'm not sure what they bonded over, if anything.

***

Dad—Allan Robert Silverstein—always looked older than he was. A teammate once asked me if my dad was my grandfather. He sported a beard and went partially bald and all gray when he was relatively young. He had a beautiful bass voice and sang in two choruses. He continued to sing until just a few months before he died at 87. His slim, athletic build meant he could rock a tux, which he wore for some of his concerts.

He was already 37 when I was born, and I think the generation gap made it difficult for us to relate to each other. He preferred classical music and opera to rock and roll. He wasn't a fan of sitcoms; he was more into PBS, which I grudgingly learned to love for his sake. I remember many Sunday nights spent watching *Masterpiece Theater* with him and my mom. And of course, he loved *Jeopardy!*, which we watched religiously as a family throughout the '80s.

Dad loved dining out and never failed to order dessert, a trait I happily inherited. Whenever he visited me in Colorado, he would take my family and me to the fanciest restaurant in Denver. It was fun to enjoy elegant meals with him. But he wasn't all about fine dining. He also loved going to Pepe's Pizzeria in New Haven, a local spot known far and wide for its wood-fired brick oven and thin crust pies. I am particularly partial to the white clam, and I still go there for a meal whenever I'm in Connecticut.

I don't think his family had much money while he was growing up. His father, Julius Silverstein, emigrated from the village of Nasheltz, Poland, to escape pogroms and poverty when he was a child. After sailing to Ellis Island, my grandfather made his way to Buffalo, where an older sister had settled. He became a United States citizen and worked for the U.S. Postal Service for many years.

My paternal grandmother, Ann Haberman Silverstein, was born in the United States. She married Jules in 1929. On their honeymoon in New York City, they attended a Yankees game. I tried to use this fact to convince my then-fiancée that we should see a Red Sox game while we were honeymooning in Vermont, but she would have none of it.

According to my dad, his father was a big sports fan who played golf, tennis and bowling.

My father was born in 1931, the oldest of three boys. He was a track star in high school. In his senior year—1948—he ran the lead leg of the 4x220-yard relay team that won the Buffalo city championship. In the same meet, he finished second in the 100-yard dash.

"He beat me by a chest," Dad said of the winner.

Dad also played football and basketball growing up and achieved the rank of Eagle Scout.

He told me once that his parents never read to him when he was a boy. He said this hurt him later, when he was in college. He eventually turned into a lover of books—especially ones by James Michener. I always remember him reading when I was young. I didn't read many books as a kid. I preferred newspapers. But I remember dad was always devouring the latest best-seller.

After I got my doctorate, I started reading for pleasure a lot more. Today, reading books brings me great joy. I also became a big fan of Michener. It just so happens that the author donated many of his papers to the University of

Northern Colorado, where I teach. The Michener Library sits right next to the building where I work. His novel *Centennial*, which is about the history of Colorado, is one of my top-three favorite books of all time. I know my father is a big reason why I love reading.

Another thing we had in common was our love of volunteering. I remember visiting him once at his studio apartment in Hamden, Connecticut, a few years before he died. One wall was almost completely covered with framed certificates from all the charity work he'd done. His example helped inspire my own community work. I was a member of the Keyette club in high school; we tutored students at Boy's Village, which still serves at-risk youth. We also helped at the annual school blood drive. I volunteered a great deal with my fraternity in college, and later in life, I became a volunteer soccer coach, taught religious school, and chaired the LGBTQ+ Task Force at my synagogue.

Dad gave blood well into his old age. I started giving in high school and still donate every eight weeks. It's an amazing feeling when I get a text saying my blood has been used to save someone's life. I guess in a way, giving blood brings me closer to my dad as well.

He was a recycler before it was cool. We used to save up the newspapers in a big pile in the furnace room. (We got three papers at one point, so it was a rather large pile.) Once the pile got big enough, my dad would tie the papers up with twine. We would load the papers and glass bottles into the car and drive to the recycling center in the next town. I guess he remembered rubber drives and metal drives during World War II. Just like my dad, I have always been a big recycler. When I lived in an apartment that didn't have a recycling service, I used to save up all the newspapers, bottles and cans to take to the local recycling center myself. It was a pain in the butt, but it was worth it to help save the environment.

My father attended a semester of college, but then the Korean War started, and he joined the Navy. An old football injury resurfaced, and the Navy gave him an honorable discharge. Instead of going about his business, he joined the Air Force. He was training as a navigator when the war ended, but he never got to serve overseas.

This training provided the groundwork for his career as a systems analyst—a computer geek. I remember going to work with him a few times when I was very young. I would bring a dot-to-dot book. I hated coloring books — too girly — but I loved my dot-to-dots. This was the 1970s, and computers were nothing like the PCs and Macs we have today. The computer took up an entire room that was kept very cold so the computer would not overheat.

Ever the recycler, he brought home used computer punch cards. I had no idea what they were until years later. We used the cards to make lists. He used to make me a list every day when I was in first grade: brush hair, brush teeth, lunch, milk money, keys. I was supposed to check off each item after I did it. For some reason, I always had trouble remembering to bring the key, despite that list, so I often ended up at the Cassidy house next door. This was nice because I had someone to hang out with, and they always seemed to have pudding in the refrigerator. I still make lists of my tasks for the day. I enjoy planning. It gives me a feeling of control. I think it helped my dad feel a sense of control as well.

My father had a lot of jobs, partly because he would periodically get mad at the boss and quit. His favorite job, by far, was in the IT department at Tiffany's. He loved riding the train into New York. He read and listened to music during the hour-plus commute. When the company moved its computer operations to New Jersey, they asked him to move, too, but he didn't want to go. He got a job running the computer network at the local hospital, instead, and he stayed there until he retired.

My father wasn't a talker. In fact, he hardly spoke at all. Trying to have a conversation with him could be downright painful. The truth is, spending time with him made me anxious. When I was young, I was never sure when he would yell at me. Anything could set him off. I especially remember him berating me when I would show emotions like sadness, anger, or disappointment. Even as an adult, I was always afraid he would fly off the handle. After I grew up and he came to visit, I would tell him I had to take a nap each afternoon, just to be alone for a while. But our mutual love of sports made our relationship bearable.

After I moved to Colorado, I used to call him once a week and we'd talk about the sports news for about five minutes. Then we'd hang up. My then-wife was amazed that our conversations were so short. But I have come to realize that those conversations, though brief, were full of love and mutual understanding. We both adored sports. And we had other things in common as well; for example, we both loved finding mistakes and calling them out. This is a trait that my ex-wife failed to appreciate in me. My father didn't have that problem. To this day, when I find a mistake in a newspaper or magazine, I feel the need to write a letter to the editor. Sometimes I just share the error on Facebook. It brings me a certain satisfaction. It makes me feel smart. And maybe it brings me closer to my dad. Perhaps that's one reason I became a copy editor.

One explanation for my dad's distinctive personality might have been hereditary. The family folklore was that his grandmother spent the last part of her life in a psychiatric hospital. His mother probably suffered from depression. I didn't know either woman, but Dad told me once that he only saw his mother smile once—for a photograph. He had his own problems with anxiety and depression. I'm glad he finally got treatment for both maladies later in life.

My dad may have suffered from generational trauma. According to my dad, Grandpa only told one story about the Old Country: He was starving and found a field of potatoes. He ate until he vomited. Then he ate more. I find this story telling. Life in Poland must have been awful. Maybe the damage was passed down.

My dad suffered from panic attacks, a trait that I unfortunately inherited. For me, it's like being overcome with a sense of dread, as if something terrible is about to happen and I'm responsible. And it can happen with the least little thing. I once had an attack when I was searching for a parking space. I've had them when deciding what to order for dinner at a restaurant. I'm glad that, unlike my dad, I got help when I was relatively young.

I know my anxiety and depression is in some part genetic, yet I can't help but think that my childhood contributed to it as well. Fear of both my parents made me scared of practically everything. Because my parents got mad at me when I shared my feelings, I turned those feelings inward. I learned not to feel.

I'm glad that my parents both worked, but that fact, coupled with the fact that my brother was six years older than me, meant I was alone for long stretches. I have always had a deep loneliness and fear of abandonment. I don't necessarily blame my parents; they did the best they knew how. But I wish they had been more accepting and more present.

My brother thinks that my dad might have been on the autism spectrum, which may be true, but I also think he was an extreme introvert. He never got along with people. Being with others sapped his energy, and he needed time alone to recharge.

I wish I had understood my father better. I wish he had understood himself better. I wish my mother had understood him. Dad did seek therapy after he and my mom divorced to get help with his anxiety and depression. But still, he always seemed unhappy.

My father may not have been good at talking, but he showed his love in different ways, like playing catch with me and attending all my games. I think he only missed one game over all my years of competition. He even showed up on crutches once after having several toenails surgically removed because of an infection.

But he didn't really know how to communicate. He would simmer and simmer and simmer and then explode. It seemed like he would yell at us just for acting like kids. I'm not sure he even liked children.

Once, when I was very young, I didn't get into the car fast enough. I can still feel the sting as he slapped me across the thigh. Or the time I started to cry and he yelled at me. Or the time I started to talk back and he yelled at me. I learned very quickly that feelings were not to be shared unless they were happy feelings. I pushed my negative feelings down, which resulted in me developing depression at a very early age.

I remember a month or two before my Bat Mitzvah, Mom and Dad wanted to hear me chant the Torah portion I would read in Hebrew in front of the congregation. I had only memorized a few of the 15 verses I was supposed to recite. Dad made me carry my substantial record collection downstairs and leave it there until after the big day. I'm not sure why this was the punishment he picked, but I was scared into submission, and I learned the rest of the Torah portion.

After my Bat Mitzvah luncheon, all the cousins and aunts and uncles came over to our house. The adults were sitting at the dining room table, talking. The kids were on the floor in the living room. We were all having a great time, fooling around. My cousin Kenny, who was about three years older than I was, was getting loud. All of a sudden, my father's voice broke through all the laughter.

"Cut the shit, Kenny!" he yelled.

The mood of the entire house immediately changed. My father had ruined our fun. And once again he had scared me.

I remember once sitting in the dining room, waiting for my mom to finish cooking dinner. She worked full-time but still did the vast majority of the cooking. She often had trouble timing the dinner; the meat and the potatoes and the vegetables never seemed to be done at the same time. I can picture myself sitting there, staring at the yellow wallpaper, potatoes and veggies growing cold, waiting for the steak. She brought it out and my dad cut it. He liked his meat well done. If it wasn't done enough for him, he'd send it back and we would have to wait until he was satisfied. Looking back now, I want to scream at him: *Why don't you cook the damn food yourself if you want it a certain way?*

One time, when I was in my early twenties, my mother and father and I went to a musical with one of Dad's friends. On the way back he wanted to stop for ice cream. I wasn't hungry. I sat there quietly while the three of them ate. He gave me dirty looks the whole time, as if my polite abstention from ice cream was somehow ruining the evening.

He didn't scream often, but we always had to be cautious because you never knew when he would explode. It wasn't just the explosions, though. It was the way he always seemed to be angry underneath whatever emotion he was showing.

Once, on one of those trips to the fancy restaurant in Denver, he had the meanest look in his eyes as he sat sipping his second cocktail after dinner. It was as if he hated me in that moment, though I never knew what for. Those looks sometimes hurt more than his yelling.

I still fear silence. My ex-wife always needed time to process things. If I would bring up something controversial, she would take a long time to respond. The silence that followed was agonizing. I feared that, like my dad, she would explode, or maybe worse, just keep silent. She never exploded, but the fear was hard to part with.

I walked on eggshells pretty much my entire childhood. Because of my father's anger. Because of his silence. And because of my mother's threats to embarrass me in public. It's one of the reasons I was depressed for so long. It's one of the reasons that when my then-wife would raise her voice, I would get scared and turn inward. Even if her anger wasn't directed toward me, I felt like I was getting in trouble—as if I were a little girl being yelled at by her parents.

Anger was natural for me for a very long time. It's how I reacted to disappointment. I would rage-kick and scream–even as an adult. Psychologists say anger is a neutral emotion. It can even be used for positive results, as when anger makes someone run for office to change things for the better. But I never knew what to do with my anger. I would lash out by screaming or throwing things. One time in college I didn't get the job I wanted at the student newspaper, and I started tossing things across my bedroom. I guess anger was always there for me, under the surface, just like it was for my dad.

Whenever I think about how bad my relationship with my father was, I remember the glue that held us together–sports–and I realize that he did have a positive impact on my life.

He liked the Mets and the Jets. I love the Red Sox and the Giants. I'm not sure why I never rooted for the teams he liked. Maybe it was my way of rebelling.

When the Mets faced the Red Sox in the World Series in 1986, our house was alive with excitement. Mom, Dad and I would sit in the basement watching the color TV, Mom in the wooden rocking chair that she nursed us in as babies, Dad in the recliner and me on the couch. Mom, who didn't really follow sports, bet me a nickel that the Mets would win.

I couldn't get enough of Clemens, Boyd, Boggs, Rice, Gedman, and Barrett. I remember exactly where I was when that ball went through Bill Buckner's legs: in the passenger seat of a van with my Burger King manager, who was driving me home from work. Incidentally, I always thought Buckner got a raw deal for that play. Not many people remember that the game was already tied when he made the error. He was a big reason the Sox were in the Series to begin with. He had 39 doubles and drove in 102 runs in 1986. And Buckner had a career to be proud of. Over 22 years, he batted .289 with more than 2,700 hits. And he had a .991 fielding percentage while playing three positions.

After the Red Sox blew Game 6, I was deflated. For the final game, I was back in the basement with Mom and Dad. It was agony. I paid Mom her nickel, then probably went to my room and cried.

I finally got my World Series win in 2004, when the Sox broke the curse of the Bambino and swept the Cardinals after coming back from a 3-0 deficit against the Yankees in the Championship Series. The first thing I did was hit my knees and thank God. The second thing I did was call Dad.

I am what you might call a Red Sox fanatic. I've got a framed, autographed Carlton Fisk jersey–the second-best present my ex ever gave me. (The first is our son.) I watch almost every game on MLB.tv. One of the items on my bucket list was to watch a game at Fenway Park with my son, and that wish came true in 2016. It was my second game at Fenway. The first came when I was about 15. My father took me, and I think we sat on the first base line. All I remember is that Gorman Thomas of the Brewers hit a home run over the Green Monster in left field, and the Red Sox lost.

The second time I went to Fenway, the Red Sox won 6-5. David Ortiz, one of the greatest Red Sox players of all time, playing in his final Major League season, hit a home run that landed about 20 yards to our left. Centerfielder Jackie Bradley Jr. made a shoestring catch that ended with a somersault. It was amazing.

My son, Darrian, who was about 10 at the time, didn't quite feel the same way. My then-fiancee, Darrian, and I had driven up from Connecticut and toured the famous sights of Boston, then had a bite to eat in the North End. As soon as we got to our seats–which were ten rows back in right field–he leaned his head on my shoulder and seemed to grow weary from the day's events. He didn't perk up until about the third inning, when he bought a bag of Cracker Jacks. He got a hot dog in the fifth. I think he appreciated the food a lot more than the play on the field. Although he played soccer when he was very young, he's not a sports fan. We never bonded over athletics. But as soon as "Take Me Out to the Ballgame" came on during the seventh-inning stretch, the three of us locked arms and sang as one. I felt like my dad was with us, too.

Some of the best times I have had over the last 19 years involve attending baseball games with Darrian. And we have played catch a few times. He hardly ever wanted to throw the ball around when I suggested it, but he would get into it after a couple of minutes. It always brought me back to my youth, with Dad in our yard fielding grounders, catching pop-ups, and seeming (at least for the moment) to be happy.

***

When I was about 12, I got a call from a coach inviting me to football practice. He said some of the kids from the baseball team were going to be there. When I arrived, the coaches were a bit surprised to see a girl. I guess they thought Lynn was a boy's name. But when they told us to take a lap around the field, I finished second, and they seemed satisfied that I could handle it. The first day of practice, the coach told us all to make sure to wear cups from then on. On the second day, the coach looked at me.

"Why aren't you wearin' a cup?"

A bunch of the kids responded, "That's a girl."

My mother sewed some foam into a training bra for extra protection in that area.

I held my own for the season, playing steadily at wide receiver and cornerback. I think I only caught one pass and made one tackle all year, but it was still some of the most fun I ever had. I loved playing football. It was loud. It was angry. It was down and dirty. It was my chance to be raw, rowdy, and roughhouse. I remember butting helmets with other players before the game to get psyched. I remember what it felt like to get tackled. I remember one drill in which we all stood in a circle. One player would stand in the middle, and the coach would call one of our names. We would run into the center and hit the guy as hard as we could.

One thing I loved about football, and all team sports, was the camaraderie. Being part of a team was not only fun, it was like being part of a family. I learned how to work with other people, some of whom I didn't particularly like. I got to know my teammates. I knew some of them weren't that talented, so I cheered extra hard when they did something well. These were great lessons that I would put into practice later in life.

I think the boys on the football team respected me. They didn't treat me differently. Never, ever did any of them ridicule me, on or off the field. After the season ended, my mother told me that one day, when I wasn't at practice, the boys got together and agreed that if anyone ever went after me, they would defend me. This might have been a bit chauvinistic, but at least they supported me. When I was playing, I didn't have time to feel like an anomaly. I was having too much fun. It was only off the field that I felt different.

The girls I was friends with probably chalked it up to Lynn being Lynn. They were used to me acting like a boy. A couple of years ago, I posted a picture of me in my football uniform on Facebook.

"You were so brave," one of my childhood girlfriends commented.

The boys on the team accepted me, and so did my friends, but I was made fun of incessantly by some of the older boys at school who weren't on the team.

There was one boy in particular. I can't remember his name, but I remember how he got right up in my face and spat: "Hey, Lynn. You gonna play football next year?" Was he going to beat me up? I wasn't sure, but I knew he didn't like the way I was acting. Inching in on his territory of maleness. His threats also made me feel shame. Shame that I was not the kind of girl that I was supposed to be. Shame that I wasn't fitting in. And he seemed to hold it against me that I would dare try to do something that up until then, no girl in my hometown had ever done.

Playing football never seemed like a big deal to me until the older boys started making fun of me. I had grown up playing baseball, so that was natural for me. My dad had nurtured my love of the game, and it brought us closer, so I stuck with it. Playing football seemed like the next logical step. My mother, ever the feminist, loved the fact that I played sports. Both my parents supported me. But when I was teased so mercilessly, I began to feel that I had crossed a line. I had wandered into territory where I didn't belong.

I loved football, but I only played one season. I quit because of the bullying; I didn't want to go through that again. And I think I was beginning to feel like I needed to act more like a girl in order to fit in. I was 13. Maybe I felt if I didn't act so masculine, boys would be attracted to me. That seemed to be the aspiration of every other teenage girl I knew, so I figured I should be wanting the same thing. I had no idea I was queer at that point. It was only years later, after I had grown up, that I realized I was denying a fundamental part of myself—not just my sexuality, but my gender queerness. But more on that later.

***

In 1972, the same year Maria Pepe filed her lawsuit against Little League, President Nixon signed Title IX into law. Most people think of sports when they think about Title IX, but it was about much more than that. The law banned sexual discrimination in schools that received federal money. This meant not only that girls could now play sports, but that they could take higher math classes and shop, which had been denied in many places. The law was groundbreaking. I was definitely a beneficiary. I not only took shop classes in seventh and eighth grade, I also played sports all through high school.

I played four sports at Joseph A. Foran High. I tried volleyball freshman year, but I was cut from the team as a sophomore. I always hated the sport after that. I played basketball for three years, lettering as a junior, but I was never very good—the kind of player the coach would send in during the final minutes to foul. I quit after junior year. I was a starter on the soccer team for two seasons, playing goalie in my junior year and forward as a senior, and I was a team captain as well. I really loved the sport and even went on to become a pretty good defender when I played years later in adult community leagues in North Carolina and Colorado.

But my best sport by far was softball. I would have rather played baseball in high school, but for some reason girls had to play softball, so that was where I ended up. I grew to love the sport, though. I started for three years at first base. I was a great bunter; I could bunt and get a hit almost anytime I wanted. But I also knew how to hit line drives. My senior year I hit .423 and won the team batting title. I still have the trophy. (No major leaguer has hit .400 since Ted Williams did it in 1941, so topping that mark is something I'm extremely proud of.) I even got to play in the senior All-Star game, with teams made up of the best players from around the state. And to think, it all started with that baseball tryout when I was eight—with a little help from Maria Pepe. But I'm not sure I would have been so successful at sports without my dad's influence. He was always there to push me and cheer me on.

***

Sports has given me so much in my life. It even gave me a trip to Europe.

My family didn't take a lot of fun vacations when I was young. I remember going to Buffalo a few times to visit relatives, and we went to Pennsylvania Dutch country once when I was very small, but there was no Disney World, no Epcot, nothing like that. So, when I got the chance to tour Europe with a soccer program between my junior and senior years of high school, I jumped at it.

There was an advertisement for a traveling team in the local newspaper, and my dad offered to take me to the tryouts. I skipped basketball practice to go. At first, I was psyched to have made Teams USA, but I later found out that all the players who tried out made it. "Teams USA" might sound like the name of a team made up of the best youth players from around the country, but we were just a bunch of kids whose parents were willing to foot the cost of a month in Europe.

Not long before the trip, there were some terrorist bombings in Europe. One of the boys in my school was supposed to go with us, but his parents got scared and canceled. I really wanted to go, and my parents decided to let me. We were told not to wear our Teams USA gear when we went into the big cities, so we tried to look like we blended in. Story of my life, I guess.

I visited the UK, the Netherlands, Belgium, France, Germany, Hungary, and Czechoslovakia. I sneaked Czech money out of the country even though it was illegal. I wonder if it's worth something now that the nation no longer exists.

We were safe, thank God, and that trip opened my eyes to a world much bigger than anything I'd ever been exposed to. We were wandering through London during a Gay Pride parade. I'd never seen anything like it before, and I was fascinated. Europe was so much more open than America, so even though I was still years away from fully embracing my gender queerness and sexuality, I was starting to see that there were ways of living that didn't conform to Connecticut's accepted norms.

***

I tried out for the softball team at Indiana, but I wasn't good enough to make a Big Ten squad. And my fear overcame me. When I visited the school in the spring of my senior year in high school, I met with the coach. She said she had enough infielders and needed outfielders. I had played mostly first base and a little shortstop in high school, but I vowed to become an outfielder. I practiced all summer, practically living at the batting cages. When it came time for walk-on tryouts in the fall, the team had a new coach. She said she had enough outfielders and needed infielders. Instead of telling her I was an infielder, I kept my mouth shut. I tried my best but didn't make the team.

So instead of playing sports in college, I became a sports journalist. I covered tennis, swimming, and baseball for the Indiana Daily Student, our campus paper. I wrote about Sergio Lopez, a swimmer from Spain who won a bronze medal in breaststroke at the 1988 Olympics. I also covered Mark Lenzi, who won the National Championship in diving for IU and a few years later went on to win Olympic gold. I wrote about Doc Counsilman, the legendary swim coach at Indiana, who once swam the English Channel and also coached Olympic gold medalist Mark Spitz. I covered All-American tennis players, wrote editorials, and served as copy desk chief.

I even got to cover an NBA game. When I was a freshman covering the women's tennis team, the sports editor of the campus paper said I was doing so well that I was eligible to cover an Indiana Pacers game. The night I was there, they played the New York Knicks. I didn't get to sit in the real press box that was right next to the court; instead, I was in the auxiliary press box, which was pretty high up. But still, I got to talk to real NBA players. I decided to interview former college star Wayman Tisdale, who had taken on a lesser role in the pros.

After the game, I waited outside the Pacers' locker room with the rest of the reporters. Then they opened the doors; and I got the shock of my life. I didn't realize that the players would be totally naked. I walked in, took one look around, and walked out. I stood outside the locker room for about five minutes hemming and hawing. I made friends with the security guard. Finally, I decided that my editor was counting on me, so I had to get my story. I went back in. Some of the players made a couple of remarks about a woman being there, but no one said anything bad. I talked to Tisdale, who by then had his boxer shorts on, and got my story. I never looked down. I even ventured into the Knicks locker room to ask Patrick Ewing what he thought about Indiana's Bob Knight, who had coached him on the Olympic team. I remember Ewing brushing his hair while laughing at my question.

"Coach Knight," he said, smirking.

That quote kind of says it all about Knight, who led Indiana to three National Championships but was not a nice human being, in my humble opinion. He was eventually fired by IU's president for mouthing off to a student. I wrote a column about the coach during my first internship, after he joked that if rape was inevitable, a woman should "relax and enjoy it." I sometimes cringe when I remember cheering him on when I was in school. But I grew up. I don't think Knight ever did.

***

I played recreational softball for a few years after graduating from college and later played tennis. That all changed when I tore my ACL. I had it repaired, but I gave up team sports after that. I ran a few miles several times a week for about five years. I have finished several 5K races and came in second in my age group in my only 10K. I loved running. It brought me joy. It was my way of meditating: Being alone with my music and my thoughts, admiring the mountains and pushing myself to be my best. I had to give up running when I developed arthritis in my foot, so now I mostly walk and work out at the gym. I recently took a boxing class, and I loved it. I have been enjoying sports all my life, and I know I have my father to thank for instilling that love of athletics in me when I was very young.

***

After college, I got a job as a copy editor at the *Connecticut Post*, a relatively large metro paper in Southern Connecticut. I started as a temporary copy editor, replacing someone who'd suffered a heart attack. My last two years there, I worked in the sports section doing a lot of story editing, layout, and headline writing. When the UConn women won their first NCAA basketball title in 1995, finishing the season undefeated, I came up with the six-column headline, "PERFECTION," with a husky dog for the "O." Once or twice a week, I would run the desk for the night. It should have been my dream job, but I was too depressed to enjoy it. I hated my boss and his red pen. Some days I was afraid to go to work and see what he'd circled from that day's paper.

Perhaps if I had been healthier, I would have applied for other jobs in sports journalism, but I was not thinking clearly. Instead, I scrapped my entire career and went back to school to study for my doctorate. I ended up becoming a journalism professor in Colorado. I'm not saying I regret getting my doctorate, but I definitely made a rather rash decision.

My Dad was very supportive when I told him my plans to return to school. He even wore a Carolina blue blazer the day I graduated with my master's from UNC-Chapel Hill. I think he was proud that I became a professor.

***

One of the ways my father and I differed was in our interpretation of religion. Dad grew up in a Conservative Jewish family that kept kosher, which means they didn't mix milk with meat and avoided shellfish and pork. They didn't eat cheeseburgers, let alone bacon cheeseburgers, which I love. He and my mom abandoned this ancient code when they had kids, but I remember that whenever we had fish for dinner, Dad would always have a glass of milk. I never understood this when I was young, but later I realized that this must have been a vestige of his youth in a kosher home. You can't have milk with beef or chicken, but you can have it with fish.

My brother and I grew up in the Reform Jewish tradition, which is more liberal. We didn't keep kosher, but we did go to services on Friday nights. I became a Bat Mitzvah, meaning I fulfilled the rituals to become an adult in the Jewish community. When I sat on the bima (the equivalent of the pulpit) that day, Dad sat next to me, as was the tradition at our synagogue. I never questioned why the father always fulfilled this role and not the mother. Looking back, I can see that it was an outdated, sexist tradition. But at the time, I just accepted it as the way things were.

After my parents divorced when I was 24 and he was 61, Dad joined a Conservative synagogue. He told me he never felt comfortable in the Reform community.

Maybe he felt like he gave up a part of himself to be with Mom. Maybe that's one of the reasons he was always angry.

But after this long-repressed burst of piety, he eventually stopped attending services altogether. Years later, he told me he wasn't sure if he believed in God.

"How can a loving God let children die?" he asked.

It's a good question. But maybe God doesn't control everything.

I think my father may have given up on God even earlier than retirement age. I remember the smell of sausage permeating the house on Yom Kippur mornings when I was young. Yom Kippur is the day Jews fast and pray all day long to atone for our sins. Not only did my dad eat on this holiest of holy days, he ate pork, which is forbidden in observant households. Although we didn't keep kosher, it was still quite a statement, as if he was giving his middle finger to the entire religion.

It might sound funny, but you don't have to believe in God to be Jewish. It's a culture as well as a religion. Many secular Jews "celebrate" Hanukkah, which isn't a religious holiday at all, by exchanging presents and eating latkes, and this makes them feel connected to their Jewish roots. Some secular Jews attend Passover Seders like the ones my family hosted when I was a kid. They can still take part, even if they don't believe in a higher being.

It makes me sad when I think about my dad losing his faith. Religion has brought me so much happiness. But each of us must choose our own path.

When I think about it now, I realize that Dad might have been *living* his religion, rather than just practicing it. One of the tenets of Judaism is *tikun olam,* which means "repairing the world" in Hebrew. All his volunteer work. Giving blood well into his 80s. Recycling. That's all part of making the world a better place.

He moved to a retirement community a couple of years before he died where they served a special Sabbath dinner every Friday night and a group met that spoke Yiddish. I guess he became a secular Jew in his old age. Maybe he always was. He seemed happy as a retiree and content with where he landed in his religion. Perhaps that's all that matters.

***

It was only as an adult that I learned something very telling about Dad.

Before he married my mother, he was engaged to a non-Jewish woman, but when he brought her home to meet his family, I guess my grandparents weren't very nice to my dad's fiancée.

"It was the coldest Thanksgiving we ever had," my Uncle Donny remembered years later.

Back then, in the 50s, it was unusual for Jews to marry outside the faith. I guess my father got the message his family was sending. He broke up with the woman and eventually married my mom. He told me several times that not marrying the love of his life was his deepest regret. It hurts to even write that. Never mind the fact that telling me that implies that he regrets marrying my mother and having my brother and me. But more than that, it reminds me of how very unhappy he always seemed when I was growing up. It came out as anger most of the time, but I know deep down he was miserable. Did he feel this way the whole time he was married to my mom? Did he regret having us kids? Did he resent us? Did the longing for his true love hinder his ability to love us as well as my mother? In some ways, I wish he would have married that woman. It would have freed both him and my mom from the perils of a terrible marriage.

***

Dad was very healthy physically for most of his life. Even in his 80s, he swam several times a week and was a member of two singing groups.

A couple of months after my wedding in 2017, Dad was diagnosed with colon cancer. He was 86 and didn't want treatment. We got the news in November, and he was dead by the first week of February. Ever the sports fan, he died on Super Bowl Sunday.

I flew to Connecticut to see him right after the diagnosis. I sat by his bed for two days but never really talked to him. I think he was still out of it from the operation in which doctors had removed most of his large intestine, but I'm not sure that's the whole story. I let my brother, who lives in New Jersey, do all the work taking care of our dad. He drove three hours to see him just about every weekend for three months. Geoff told me at one point that I needed to come in March, when he was going to be out of town. I made a reservation, but Dad died before that date rolled around.

One thing I did do for my dad in his last days was call him. Before he got sick, I would usually call him every Sunday. After he got sick, I'd call several times a week. At least I was there in that way.

But I never visited after that one time.

Even now, years later, I sometimes wonder why I wasn't there for him at the end. Why didn't I visit him when he got to the nursing home? Why didn't I visit him when he entered hospice?

Maybe it's because, although he was there for me when I was young, he wasn't really *there* for me. He was present physically, attending ballgames and other events, but he wasn't there for me emotionally. He couldn't deal with my feelings, probably because he couldn't deal with his own feelings. Emotions made him uncomfortable. But he made me uncomfortable, too. It was so difficult to be around him. Maybe that's why I put off going; I didn't want to deal with that anxious silence—that space between us that needed to be filled with something … something I could never put my finger on … something intangible that was never there between us except when we were playing catch or watching a ballgame. I wish I had been able to fill that space.

Maybe it has to do with the fact that when I shared my feelings of anger or sadness as a kid, my father rejected me. I don't think I ever got over my hurt from those rejections.

I think another reason I didn't visit him was that I was afraid I would have to talk to him–really talk to him. We never talked about how he acted during my childhood. I was still afraid of him as an adult, so I never confronted him about it. I don't regret that part of it. I needed to be safe. I didn't want to open myself to his anger.

But anger was far from the only emotion my dad felt. He found joy in things like sports, music and volunteering.

And even as he got sicker and sicker, he continued to enjoy *Jeopardy!* every night, even when he was in hospice. I wish so much that he could have seen me on the show, but he died about a month and a half before my episodes aired.

After I taped the show, he joked that I couldn't tell him how I did for penalty of death and said that he probably wouldn't get to see it anyway. I guess I was hoping this wasn't true, because I didn't tell him I had won until the day he died. My brother called to let me know that Dad wasn't doing well, so I called the nursing home and asked if the nurse could put the phone up to his ear. I told him I loved him, and then I blurted something else out: "I won *Jeopardy! $10,000!*"

I don't know if he heard or not. I wish I had told him earlier.

It's hard to believe I danced with my dad at my wedding, and less than six months later he was dead. I'm glad I got to have that dance. I only wish my mom could have lived long enough to have been there as well.

***

Besides anger, anxiety and depression, another thing my dad and I had in common was cancer. I was lucky. I survived.

I was diagnosed when I was 53, in late July of 2022. You might say my primary care physician saved my life. After I underwent a routine blood test a week before bunion surgery, my PCP emailed me to say my calcium level was high. She said to get another test in a month, so that's what I did. She sent another email saying the calcium level was still high and she was referring me to an oncologist because high calcium can be a sign of malignancy.

The oncologist, Dr. Britt, performed a quick physical exam and told me he didn't think there was anything wrong with me, but that he would order a CT scan just to make sure. So I had the scan. A few days later, Dr. Britt called.

"You have a mass on your liver."

I was shocked. I had always considered myself the healthiest person I knew. I ate hardly any red meat and subsisted mostly on fresh fruits, vegetables and whole grains. I had given up drinking several years earlier and didn't do drugs. My only downfall was my sweet tooth.

But here I was, staring a cancer diagnosis in the face. It was cancer of the bile ducts, so it involved the liver and gallbladder.

I was scared. Check that. I was petrified. Luckily, my wife was there the whole time, even though we had started the divorce process. She accompanied me to all my appointments and procedures and stayed at the hospital during my eventual surgery.

The first thing we did was consult with the tumor board. A tumor board is a group of physicians and nurses who work together to figure out the best way to treat a patient's cancer.

The day started in the morning with a visit to a nurse practioner, who performed a quick exam. Then I had blood drawn. (This was a sign of things to come, as for the next year I pretty much became a living pin cushion. The good thing is that I have such a great vein on my right arm that phlebotomists salivate when they see it, so it never hurt.)

After lunch in the hospital cafeteria – I'm pretty sure I had chicken noodle soup – we saw the doctors. First came the surgeon. He was a liver specialist who performed transplants as well as cancer surgery. He said that I definitely needed an operation. He also said it was a good thing the liver regenerates, because if it didn't, "we'd be trying to make you comfortable." He also mentioned the possibility of a liver transplant if worse came to worst, but I didn't have time to really process that because before the surgeon even left, in walked the radiologist, Dr. Lindquist. He told me that before the surgeon could operate, he had to shrink the tumor and at the same time enlarge the healthy part of my liver. He would do that by placing millions of tiny, radioactive glass beads in my liver through the femoral artery.

The radiation came in October. I underwent this procedure twice. The first time was a dry run with slightly radioactive beads. The second time, which occurred about three weeks after the first, I was told not to stand too close to small children or older adults for a few days. There was a Geiger counter in the operating room. Dr. Lindquist said I would probably hate him for about two weeks. He prescribed Oxycodone, and I steeled myself for the worst.

What followed was not two weeks but six weeks of the worst pain I have ever experienced. I kept calling the doctor's office for more Oxy, but it had no effect. Although I hadn't smoked weed in years, I seriously considered using edibles. Then a friend told me about CBD, which is made from marijuana but doesn't get you high. It helped a little. The only thing that alleviated the pain—at least for a few minutes—was a bath or a shower, so I took several each day.

When I went back to see Dr. Lindquist a week before my surgery, he told me that most people who have a massive dose of radiation like me experience pain for six weeks.

"We basically set off a nuclear bomb in your liver."

I wished he had told me that six weeks earlier.

He also told me that the reason he'd given me such a massive dose of radiation was that – except for the tumor on my liver–I was extremely healthy.

During the one pain-free week before my operation, I visited the surgeon. It was a different doctor than the one we saw with the tumor board–her name was Kendra Conzen, and she was also a liver specialist. She proceeded to tell me all the things that could go wrong. It was a long list – everything from waking up with a drain in my abdomen to waking up in the ICU to not waking up at all.

I broke down in sobs. Dr. Conzen tried to comfort me. She went to find some tissues. I'm glad my wife was there.

The bottom line was that Dr. Conzen was going to remove two-thirds of my liver, as well as my gallbladder. She said it should be okay because, as long as I was left with at least twenty-five percent of my liver, I'd be able to survive. I guess having thirty-four percent of a liver's not so bad. And as the original surgeon had told me, the liver regenerates, so if everything went as planned, by the next year I would be good as new.

On November 30, 2022, Dr. Conzen operated on me for seven-and-a-half hours. She told me later that she had to use a chisel-like tool because the radiation had damaged my liver so badly that it was stuck to the surrounding organs. But she also told me that she removed all of the cancer, including the margins, so I was pretty much cured.

I spent seven nights in the hospital. It was horrible. The thing about being in the hospital is that you have no control. I couldn't even go to the bathroom by myself.

And the whole time I felt like I'd been run over by a truck.

When I got home, my wife stayed with me for one night before my brother arrived from New Jersey to look after me for the next few days. He was wonderful. He shopped, cooked, and even cleaned a little. I was upset because I couldn't host my annual Hanukkah party, so we invited his son, who lives in Denver, to join us. Geoff prepared latkes as I supervised. He also made steak and applesauce. That night, my brother, my nephew, my son and I celebrated not just the rededication of the ancient Temple in Jerusalem, but my survival as well. I will always be thankful for Geoff's loving kindness at this trying time.

About six weeks after the surgery, I started chemotherapy. It was done purely as a precaution, just in case there were any cancer cells still lurking in my body. Because it was oral chemo, it wasn't as bad as the intravenous kind, but it was still one of the toughest things I ever went through. Dr. Britt prescribed a relatively high dose at first. I had diarrhea so bad that for about two weeks, the only thing I could stomach was marshmallows. The doctor lowered the dose, and I was able to eat again. But then I lost my fingerprints. I'm not kidding. I lost my fingerprints. I could no longer open my i-Phone or my laptop with my thumb or index finger. I had to punch in the code. It was annoying, but at least I was alive.

Other side effects included terribly dry skin on the souls of my feet and the palms of my hands. My feet peeled so badly that pieces of skin would come off when I walked. And for a while I had no sense of taste. I would make something that usually thrilled me, but it tasted like nothing. The only thing I could taste was sweet, so I ate a lot more marshmallows.

I finished the chemotherapy in early August of 2023, so my cancer ordeal lasted about a year. I would say that's pretty good compared to many other people's battles.

I had CT scans every few months for the first two years following the surgery. I saw Dr. Britt recently, and he said I'll need annual scans for the next three years. He also told me that if the cancer was going to return, it probably would have already.

After surviving cancer, I decided to treat myself to ice cream at my favorite place once a week every summer. It's a way to remember my battle and confirm that I am a warrior who can get through just about anything. And I don't worry about eating too much dessert, no matter the season. After coming so close to death, I decided that life's too short to live without sweets.

I also celebrated my victory over the disease with a tattoo featuring the green bile duct/liver cancer ribbon emblazoned with the word "survivor" on my upper left arm.

But there's always the chance my cancer will return, and I live with that reality every day. At first it was tough. I was getting undressed one night and felt a lump in my armpit, and I freaked out. I made an appointment with Dr. Britt, who told me it wasn't anything to worry about.

After a couple of years of being healthy, I don't fear cancer's return as much as I once did, but I don't think I'll ever get over the ordeal. When you have cancer, it's like your own body is trying to kill you. That's not an easy thing to deal with.

***

I wonder now what my dad was thinking when he was dying of cancer. I had no problem with the fact that he didn't want to treat it. He was 86 when he was diagnosed. That's a long life. It wasn't an easy life, but he muddled through.

He wasn't perfect, but he was a good father in many ways. He passed down his love of sports, which helped me learn how to be part of a team. That in turn taught me how to play fair and how to work with people of all abilities. I will always be grateful for that. He taught me to love reading. He encouraged me to try new things, especially when it came to food. And I remember the look on his face when I modeled my Bat Mitzvah dress for him. I know he loved me, and he told me so often.

But he also taught me how to hold in my feelings. How to yell and scream when I didn't get my way. I resented him for years.

No parent is all bad or all good. You take the positives and the negatives, and you make a life, and that is what I have done. It took me years to be able to deal with my anger in a less destructive way. Now that I've figured it out, I am able to appreciate all that Dad gave me.

I played tackle football for one year and loved every minute of it.

4

Swarm of Dykes

The first time I remember meeting Uncle Donny was at my brother's Bar Mitzvah, when I was 7. I didn't see him again until my brother's first wedding, when I was 19. The last time I saw him was at my son's Bar Mitzvah in 2018, when I was almost 50. We didn't spend a lot of time together, but in the last few years of his life, we became close. I didn't realize it until much later, but Uncle Donny was my biggest role model for how to live life out and proud. The only problem was that I didn't really know him until I grew up, so I didn't get to have him as a role model until later in life.

I remember driving with the family from Connecticut to Buffalo several times when I was young to visit my dad's middle brother, Uncle Jackie, and his wife and daughters. They visited us several times, as well. But we never saw Uncle Donny. My father and his youngest brother didn't see each other much. This might have been because he lived in California, but I don't think my father spoke to him much on the phone, either.

Communication was not something the Silversteins did well. I remember my mom telling a story once that my dad had sent Donny a hooked rug that he'd made. Uncle Donny didn't send a thank-you note. When my dad complained, Uncle Donny, a pharmacist, sent a terse note on the back of a prescription slip. This story may have been apocryphal; my mother tended to exaggerate. But the fact remains that although my uncle lived in a committed, loving relationship with another man for over 40 years, the lack of communication between my dad and my uncle left me without a queer role model for most of my youth.

My parents didn't really talk about Uncle Donny when I was growing up. My mother and Donny had been friends when they were young, and I remember my mom being upset with him over the years for different reasons. I also remember my mother telling me that Uncle Donny must have been gay because when Uncle Jackie visited, he yelled at my dad.

"You don't let your kids say 'shit', but you let them say 'faggot!'" Jackie had said.

That was years before I had any inkling that I was queer, but I knew I was different from an early age. As a teenager, I fantasized about having sex with women, but I never thought that you could really have a relationship with someone of the same sex. I may have internalized some homophobia from both my parents. They were rather liberal; they let me dress like a boy and play every sport imaginable, but I somehow believed deep inside that it was wrong to be attracted to girls.

As I grew up, I noticed that all the other girls were developing crushes on boys. In about fifth grade, I picked out a boy and decided he was kind of cute, so I developed a "crush" on him. He was the smartest boy in the class, and he wasn't mean to me like some of the other boys were. I had a "crush" on him for a few years. Looking back, I didn't really know what a crush was at that point. A few of my friends had boyfriends, but I never did. When I got to high school, I still didn't really like boys, although I had a few more "crushes." And none of the boys seemed the least bit interested in me, which made me sad but was probably a blessing in disguise.

Despite my lack of a boyfriend, I did go to my junior prom. I asked my friend Bryan to go with me, purely platonically. (He had a girlfriend.) He went to another school, so he set me up with his friend Charlie, who needed a date to *his* prom, which was scheduled about a month before mine. I was so excited—my first date! Unfortunately, Charlie's prom was not much fun. Maybe it was Charlie who wasn't much fun, though his friends were nice. Still, I was relieved to have a reciprocal date in place for my own dance.

Then Charlie called a week before the big night. I was so excited to hear from him.

"I've got some bad news," he told me. "I have this family reunion next week, and I won't be able to go to the prom with you."

I was devastated. I felt like a laughingstock. Who gets stood up for prom? *Not real girls.*

But my friend Bryan came through, escorting me after all.

Boring Charlie's prom still turned out to be positive overall, because one of those nice people I'd met became my first boyfriend. His name was Andy, and he was very sweet.

One evening, after we had been going out for about three months, we were making out in my car, in front of his house.

And then he dropped the bomb: "I love you."

I said the only thing I could think of to say: "I'm not gonna marry you!"

I broke up with him soon after that.

I admit my reaction was a bit over the top, but I had no idea how relationships worked. I figured if a guy loved you, you had to marry him. And I certainly didn't want that.

I met my second boyfriend in my first year at Indiana. I guess he was more like a guy I dated for a month than a boyfriend. But when he started hinting about sex, I began to act horribly toward him. It worked. He got mad and stopped calling me. I never let a man get close to me–either emotionally or physically.

I had crushes on a couple of my female professors, but I pushed these feelings down and pretended to be straight. I doubt I was fooling anyone. I mean, one look at me and you could tell. I think the only person who didn't know I was gay was me.

Around that same time, I met my Uncle Donny's partner, Jon. It was 1988, and I had just finished my freshman year of college. The big family event of that summer was Geoff's wedding, and Donny and Jon had flown out from California to attend.

I didn't think much of it at the time, but a few years later—after I had finally caught up with everyone else's conclusions about me and realized that I was gay—I nervously called them to ask if my girlfriend and I could stay with them for a few days while we were visiting the West Coast.

Uncle Donny laughed. "We *thought* you were gay when we met you at the wedding!"

If only I'd known Donny and Jon when I was young, I might have understood the feelings I'd had about girls. When I was in high school, I flirted with girls, but I didn't know I was flirting. I just thought I was being friendly. I didn't realize what I was feeling was a real, honest-to-goodness crush—not that pretend stuff I made up to fit in. I had no idea I was gay. Well, I had some idea, but I suppressed it. Whenever I'd fantasize about sex, I'd think of myself as a man with a woman. But I never put two and two together. I just didn't have anything to compare it to.

There were no role models back then. The only lesbian I'd ever heard of was Martina Navratilova, and she was the foil to my favorite tennis player, Chris Evert. Today I think of Martina as a hero, but back then she was the "other." She was everything I didn't want to be—manly, bold, obvious in her "otherness." Years later, when someone I worked with made fun of Martina for being butch, I shivered inside, hoping he didn't think I was that way. And as for transgender or nonbinary role models, forget about it. Even if those words existed when I was a kid, I never heard them used.

I remember in grammar school, kids used to say that anyone who wore pink and green on Thursday was gay. I'm not sure I even knew what "gay" meant, but I knew it wasn't something I wanted to be. It was just some dumb, arbitrary "rule" some prepubescent kid came up with 40 years ago, but I still think of this when I wear pink and green together.

My mom used to refer to Jon as her "sister-in-law." I laughed it off when I was young, but looking back now, I realize how hurtful this was. Was Jon not a real man because he was gay?

You can try to brush off my mother's remark by saying that some gay men refer to each other with feminine terms, but I have a big problem with that. When an LGBTQ+ person uses what might seem like a derogatory term for themselves or another queer person, they are taking back the disparaging word and using it in a way that gives them power. It's an act of reclaiming. When a straight person does it, it's insensitive, unkind, and disrespectful. It further perpetuates the hurtfulness.

My mother's behavior toward Donny and Jon gave me the distinct impression she would not welcome a lesbian daughter into her life. There were other hints, too.

A kid I carpooled to Hebrew school with when I was young later came out as gay. His mother ended up dying by suicide. My mom said that she probably killed herself because her son was gay.

Once, when I was in my early 20s, I asked her what she would do if *I* were gay.

"I'd be sad for you."

Years later, she said she'd only meant that she'd feel sorry for me because I'd miss out on a wedding and being a mom. (Little did she know at that time that I would someday have both a wedding and a son.) But I took it as if she thought being gay itself was something to feel sad about.

I didn't realize until much later in life that even if your mother is a liberal feminist who encourages you to play sports and dress like a boy, she can still be homophobic.

Yet despite all of this, my mom embraced me when I came out. She joined the local P-FLAG chapter and marched in the Pride Parade. She accepted me and loved me. But the cruel things she said when I was young still cut me to the core.

It wasn't just the homophobic things my mom said that affected me. It was the lack of any discussion about homosexuality in the larger world. It was never talked about. It was like it didn't exist. I often wonder why, when we tell children about sex, we don't also tell them that there are other ways to love someone than being straight. The proverbial "sex talk" is all about making babies, not relationships, love, or even just enjoyment. Gay men and lesbians don't fit that baby-making scenario, so they get left out.

***

When I was a sophomore at Indiana, I went to a party and met a nice woman. We hung out all night and had a great time. It was cold, so I let her wear my jacket. At some point we went into town to buy more liquor for the party. She said she had to make a quick stop. I remember sitting outside a nightclub for what seemed like a rather long time. I knew it was a gay bar, but I didn't really want to think about what that meant: what it meant for her, and what it meant for me because I was hanging out with her. Maybe she was trying to tell me something by stopping there with this naive kid who had no idea she herself was queer.

The next day, I found a note in my jacket pocket.

"I had a really nice time hanging out with you. Call me sometime."

I was disgusted. Did she think I was gay?

***

During my senior year in college, I went to a couple of meetings of a lesbian support group. I had never even kissed a girl, but I wanted to find out if what I'd been feeling for so long was real. I was yearning to come out, but it still didn't feel right.

There was a woman who worked at the student newspaper with me who was out. I talked to her a few times about what I was feeling. She was very supportive. I also told another friend. I don't remember her exact reaction, but she told me years later that it was not very welcoming.

I remember sitting in the office of one of the journalism faculty members—I think she was the placement director. I was depressed, or maybe I was having a panic attack, or maybe both. The point is, I wasn't in a good place, and I guess she thought I was ripe for indoctrination. She asked if she could shut the door. She told me about how when she was in college and playing a lot of basketball, she was hanging out with a lot of lesbians. She said she started hearing voices speaking some weird language, and she repeated what seemed (to me) like crazy, made-up words that you would hear at a revival meeting when people speak in tongues.

"God doesn't want you to be a lesbian," she finally told me.

I was stunned. Having grown up Jewish, I was a bit wary of Christianity. I had heard this type of thing took place; I had seen "Brother Max," as he was known, who preached on campus several times a year, but I'd never experienced this type of proselytization before. I quietly excused myself and left. I never told anyone at IU what happened. I'm sure this woman could have gotten into major trouble for what she'd done. But I was too embarrassed to bring it up with university officials. After all, if I told someone, people might think I was gay.

Coupled with the homophobia I had internalized from my parents and what I saw every day in society, this experience further convinced me that being gay was wrong, so I kept pushing it down.

***

When I started working at a newspaper after college, I met a man who seemed interested in me. He was an alcoholic, pot-smoking loser who had lost his license to drunk driving, but he was interested in me, so I went out with him. Again, I was trying to fit in. I spent three years dating him, on and off, even though the whole time I knew I was queer. I'm pretty sure he knew, too. I was getting ready to come out. I just needed to find a way.

I finally came out when I was twenty-six and about to begin graduate school. Maybe it was because I was moving to North Carolina for school, so I could start fresh. I wouldn't have to hang out with old friends who might not accept the "new" me.

I came out to my mom first. She was very supportive. And she wasn't surprised.

"I think I'm … I think I am."

That's all I could say. I couldn't even bring myself to say the word "gay."

Her response didn't surprise me.

"I kind of knew."

Well, that was easy.

Once her suspicions were confirmed, true to her nature, my mom didn't mind telling anyone she met that her daughter was a lesbian.

I remember once she told me a story about a woman she'd met at her synagogue in Connecticut. I was living in Chapel Hill, North Carolina, at the time, and the woman suggested I meet up with her son who lived in the area. My mother said it probably wasn't a good idea. The woman persisted. My mother tried to be kind. Finally, the woman blurted out the gist of the situation.

"He's looking for a nice Jewish girl."

Without missing a beat, my mother shot back:

"So is my daughter."

I told my dad I was gay the first time he visited me in North Carolina.

He didn't say much at first, but as I was about to drop him off at the airport, he got serious: "I still love you."

After waiting all that time to come out, I was embraced by my parents. I guess it was me who wasn't willing to accept who I was for all those years.

***

After moving to Chapel Hill, I began exploring my sexuality. I started hanging out at a gay bar in Raleigh that hosted a women's night on Thursdays. I almost immediately developed a crush on a woman who claimed she had a girlfriend but always went to the bar alone. She was the first woman I ever kissed. It was heavenly. I guess it had to be, considering I'd waited until I was nearly twenty-seven years old to try it.

A few weeks after my first kiss, I met a woman at the bar. Her name was Bridgette. She lived in West Virginia and was in town for work. We hit it off. I followed her back to her hotel room. We spent the night together. It was heavenly … although I'm not sure I had any idea what I was doing.

With sex out of the way, I began to look for my first girlfriend. I put an ad in a local independent newspaper, but nothing came of it except a rendezvous with a woman who used the "N" word on our second and last date.

I soon realized there was one other lesbian in my class, so of course we hooked up. It should have ended after one night, but I'm what you might call a "serial monogamist," and it turned into a not-so-great relationship that lasted a couple of months. When she broke up with me, I went a bit nuts. I wandered around campus for a couple of hours and ran into one of my professors, who took me to the student health center. I stayed the night. The nurse asked me if she needed to take my belt. I told her I would be fine. I checked out the next day and went to class. All the other students seemed to know what had happened. It was embarrassing, but in a way, it was also nice to have all eyes on me. I was very sick at this time.

Soon after my first relationship ended, I started searching for girlfriend number two. I answered an ad in the independent paper and met Lisa. Her ad said something about appreciating both Frank Sinatra and Nirvana. I was not a fan of Sinatra, but I called her anyway. The relationship lasted for three years. I'm not sure she even liked me; I think she might have just been afraid to tell me the truth. After dating for two years, we decided to try to do the long-distance thing when I moved to Athens, Ohio, to get my doctorate. That lasted about a year, and I told her I couldn't do it anymore.

Looking back, I'm not sure what Lisa and I ever had in common. She was adamantly against having children, and I loved kids. This should have been a deal breaker from the start, but I didn't care. I just wanted a partner. I didn't want to feel alone the way I had as a kid. I would repeat this cycle again and again for many years.

I think one of the things that precipitated my break-up with Lisa was my involvement with the activist group Swarm of Dykes.

During my first semester at Ohio University, I worked part time critiquing the student newspaper. I really enjoyed this work; it combined my love of news, my affinity for editing, and a bit of teaching. Early in my second semester, I lost the job. I'm not sure exactly what happened. All I remember is that I pointed out a badly worded photo caption. The caption referred to a ballgame of some kind which Ohio U had lost. It said something like "Bobcats outplayed, out [something], just outed." I told the editing team that "outed" implied that the players were all gay. One of the women at the newspaper told me after that meeting that someone in her family was gay and that the rest of the editors did not want to hear anything about the subject. I was fired a few days later. I'm pretty sure this was the impetus for my joining Swarm of Dykes.

Swarm of Dykes was founded a semester before I got to OU by a group of undergrads who were tired of the homophobia and sexism they were seeing in Athens. The name was a way of taking back a word that had been used against lesbians for many years, claiming it as our own so we could hold the power for once. The organization—made up of lesbians, one or two gay men, some transgender men, and a few allies—was a grassroots group seeking to shine light on these problems. We staged in-your-face events like handing out "cunt coloring books" and served as guards on the Take Back the Night march. We even had a rec softball team called "Dykes on Spikes." I still have my jersey.

I had a lot of fun in Swarm of Dykes. It was just the thing I needed at that time in my life. I had missed out on being out while I was an undergrad, so this was my chance to make some noise. Graduate school is where I found myself, and Swarm of Dykes was a big part of that.

When I started participating in events with Swarm of Dykes, I told Lisa about it, eager to hear what she had to say. I told her that Swarm of Dykes was based on the Lesbian Avenger groups that were popular at that time. Her response was a game changer: "I don't like their tactics."

Although there were signs all through our relationship that she wasn't the one for me, I think this moment was when I knew it wasn't going to work. Lisa was still pretty much in the closet. She had told her older sister that she was gay, but she kept the rest of the family in the dark, and none of her work colleagues knew. She grew up Baptist in a small Southern town, so I can understand how difficult it must have been for her. But I was living out and proud, and Lisa's closeted attitude didn't really fit into my life. I was making friends. I was participating in direct actions and (I hope) making a difference. Swarm of Dykes gave me the confidence to do things I never thought I could do; it finally gave me a voice.

Like most college campuses, Ohio University attracted preachers who would try to "save" the students. One of these preachers showed up on campus not long after I joined Swarm of Dykes. He would accost students on the green across from the student union during lunchtime. He wasn't just preaching; he was saying nasty things about people with no grounds for any of his claims. For instance, if he saw a woman smoking, he would imply that she probably gave oral sex. A bunch of my friends from Swarm of Dykes and I got fed up and decided to do something. One day, I parked my car right next to where this guy was spewing his hate speech, climbed up on top of the car, and started shouting about how he was not a man of God—that he was a charlatan and a loser. A huge crowd gathered. Someone took a photo that ended up in the local paper. I felt like I was on top of the world.

Some of the most fun I had with Swarm of Dykes was eating fire. I think it was after the Take Back the Night march. We did it to "take back the power" that had been stolen from us by the patriarchy and heterosexism, but for me, it was also about taking back the power that was stolen from me by my parents, who scared me and never let me feel my feelings when I was young. I was taking back the power from the bullies who had made fun of me when I was young because I didn't look or act like a girl. I wanted to feel, physically, all the power that had been stripped from me, so when the opportunity came to try fire-eating, I was all in.

Eating fire may look dangerous, but it's not really that hard. The moisture in your mouth puts out the fire. True, your mouth tastes like kerosine the rest of the night, but you feel empowered—almost invincible—afterward.

Swarm of Dykes also sponsored a talent night each year. I participated twice. The first year, I performed a spoken-word rendition of Bruce Springsteen's "Thunder Road," which was very well-received. The next year, I lip-synched to a mix tape I put together. I remember changing outfits several times during the performance. I kept taking layers off until I was wearing a midriff-baring top and short shorts as *I Feel Pretty* from *West Side Story* played. This was the ultimate in drag for me. I was a woman who strutted around like a man, pretending to be a girly-girl.

During my time with Swarm of Dykes, I began calling myself a "Jewish American Dyke." I guess it was a play on the "Jewish American Princess," which was a big thing in the 1980s. There were all kinds of jokes about "JAPs." A few folks in the Swarm started calling me "JAD."

A friend of mine who was also a member of Swarm of Dykes used to lead services for students during Coming Out Week. She titled these events "Coming Out Christian." Taking my cue from her, I started leading events for queer Jewish students. Once I even gave a sermon about being queer and Jewish. The

Torah portion that week was Noah's Ark, so I talked about how the rainbow symbolized both a covenant with God and a symbol for queer pride.

Years later, after my mom died, I decided to get my first tattoo. I'm not sure what the impetus was for this; my mom had always hated tattoos. She maintained that Jews weren't supposed to get them. I know it's in the Bible, but the Bible also says a man shouldn't lie with a man and that you shouldn't eat pork, and my mother had no problem with either of those things. Is being a bacon cheeseburger-loving queer person any different than being a bacon cheeseburger-loving queer person with a tattoo?

It took me a couple of years to figure out the design for the tat. At some point I focused on Judaism. I wanted to tell people who I was. It came to me one day that what I am is a queer Jew, so I decided on a rainbow star of David on my upper right arm. It was my way of showing the world that I was proud not only of my Jewish heritage, but of my queerness as well. I've gotten many compliments on the tat over the years. A lot of people regret their tattoos later in life. I don't think I ever will. It's me in a nutshell. How could I ever regret who I am?

***

When my then-fiancée and I were planning our wedding in 2017, we knew we wanted it to be an intimate affair. She doesn't have a big family, and I'm not close with my extended family. We decided to invite only about thirty relatives and friends, total. After we sent out the invitations, I got an email from Uncle Donny and Jon: "Aren't we invited?"

Diana and I agreed that it would be wonderful if they attended. I had thought about including them on the guest list, but because I wasn't inviting any other extended family, I'd decided against it.

Once they asked, however, I realized how much sense it made to have them there. I mean, why *wouldn't* I invite my gay uncle and his longtime partner to my lesbian wedding?

They took the two of us out for pizza a couple of days before the ceremony, and afterward we played hearts at our condo. It was lovely hanging out with them. It was that night that I found out that Donny and Jon had finally gotten married. Donny said he wasn't sold on the idea at first, but after thinking about it, he came around.

"Love is love," he said.

***

My father got sick a couple of months after the wedding, and he died a few months later. It was tough not having him and my mother at my son's Bar Mitzvah, which was a couple of months after that.

The synagogue we belonged to at that time had a tradition of symbolically handing the Torah–the holy scroll we read during services–down from the grandparents to the parents to the Bar Mitzvah child. As the big event drew closer, I was thinking to myself that I didn't want to even do this because both my parents were dead and my son's other parent wasn't Jewish. But when we met with the rabbi about a month before the ceremony, he presented it in such a way that it seemed doable.

My ex's mother was going to be at the Bar Mitzvah, so it was a no-brainer that she would take part in the symbolic passing of the Torah. I figured his birth mom should also be included.

I began thinking of who could possibly take part from my family. My brother seemed like a good fit. Then I had an epiphany. Why not Uncle Donny?

He was never one for talking on the phone, so I sent him an email. I told him that he'd been a role model for me for a long time. He'd been with his husband for almost 40 years at that point, and although he wasn't a part of my life when I was a kid, his long commitment to Jon taught me that gay relationships can last.

Uncle Donny agreed to take part in the Torah passing, and I think that had a positive effect on our relationship. After the Bar Mitzvah, we started texting. I found out that we were both big fans of the Boston Red Sox, so at first, we talked about that. It turned into a real friendship. He would text me silly jokes he thought up in the shower. I would text him about sports. I really enjoyed finally getting to know him.

Uncle Donny died about three years after the Bar Mitzvah.

A couple of weeks before he died, I asked him if he had gotten along with his brothers when they were young. He said it was always either Donny and Jackie or Allan and Jackie, never Donny and my dad. Their eight-year age-difference may have contributed, but I got the sense that my dad just never fully accepted Donny for who he was.

Then I asked him if he ever came out to his parents. He said he had not because he was a "late bloomer." Both my paternal grandparents died relatively young, when Uncle Donny was in his mid-thirties.

I texted him the morning of the Super Bowl LV, but I never got an answer. He was a big Tom Brady fan, and Brady was playing in his 10th title game that night (and his first with Tampa Bay), so I wondered why he didn't text back. Jon called later that day to tell me Uncle Donny had suffered a brain hemorrhage.

I cried more on the phone with Jon that day than I did when I found out my dad had cancer. Maybe it's because my relationship with my dad always felt a little forced. It was so difficult to talk to him. All the hurt from things he did when I was young clouded the conversations we had after I became an adult. With my uncle, it was just fun. I hadn't really known him when I was young, so there was no baggage, and he had always been fully accepting of exactly who I was.

My grief around Uncle Donny's death was complex. There was a lot of symbolic loss alongside the literal loss. He had the stroke on Super Bowl Sunday; my dad had died three years earlier, also on Super Bowl Sunday. Uncle Donny also died seven years to the day that my mom died. Of course that's just coincidence, but I can try to make sense out of it, nonetheless. I think back to how my uncle stood in for my parents when we passed down the Torah at the Bar Mitzvah. And I think about how he really was a role model for me. I think about him particularly when I watch the Red Sox play their chief rival, the New York Yankees. How I wish I could text him during those games.

And then I think about how, although they loved me very much and tried their best, my parents were sometimes lacking in the things that needed to be done to make me feel safe when I was young. And I think that maybe, after my parents died, Uncle Donny filled in for them. I'm not saying he acted like a parent. He didn't. But I think he gave me the unconditional love I never got from my mom and dad. It took me a long time to figure out how important he was to me, but once I found him, I cherished our relationship. And now that he's gone, I miss him dearly. And I only hope that someday I can have the kind of relationship that he and Jon had for all those years.

Living out and proud has helped me learn to love myself. But there were still other things I needed to do to really become my true self. I was getting closer, but I still wasn't quite there yet.

Me at the Joseph A. Foran High School Junior Prom in 1986. My date canceled on me a week before the big night, but my friend came through and escorted me.

My high school yearbook photo. I still love pink.

My parents at my brother's wedding in 1988.

5

Serenity, Courage, Wisdom

I am sitting in Pepe's Pizzeria in New Haven, Connecticut, with my family. I am about six.

My father has ordered a draft beer. The foam fascinates me.

"Can I drink the bubbles?"

My dad, who always had a hard time telling me no, obliges.

Those bubbles taste like nothing I've ever had before. And I feel like one of the grown-ups. After that, whenever my dad orders a draft beer, I get to drink the bubbles.

***

I was an odd little kid. I sucked my thumb and carried around a baby blanket until I was about 10. Not in school or around friends or anything like that; but when I was with family, my blanket and thumb were soothing. The thumb-sucking was so bad that I ended up with prominent buck teeth, which were eventually fixed with braces. My blanket was a disgusting yellow corner of one of my older brother's blankets, so I called it "Corner Blanket." I wonder what it says about my family that I needed that feeling of security when I was with them.

I remember when we went to visit Geoffrey at sleepaway camp when I was about eight or nine. We were walking in the woods when my Uncle Ronny (who technically wasn't an uncle but was close friends with my parents) told me to throw it away, so I did. A few hours later, I told everyone that we had to go back to the woods to get Corner Blanket. The adults were quite disappointed, but I needed that blanket. I did find it, thankfully.

I was afraid for much of my childhood. Afraid of my parents, afraid of people I didn't know, afraid to make a mistake, afraid of practically everything. I think the only place I was never afraid was on the ball field. Sucking my thumb and carrying around Corner Blanket helped alleviate these fears when I wasn't playing ball.

When I was in grade school, I was bullied by a boy in my class. Whenever we were on the playground, he would call me "monkey" and make screeching noises. This went on every day, and the teachers never seemed to notice or care. I guess back then, in the early 1980s, adults thought this type of thing built character. It just made me feel more inadequate. Like there was something wrong with me. Like I was unworthy of love and acceptance.

I was always a part of the group, but I never felt like I fit in. Always on the outside, looking in. When I was in my early teens, a friend from day camp invited me to a meeting of B'nai B'rith Girls, a group for Jewish teens. We were doing an activity in which a candle was passed from person to person as we sat in a circle. When it reached you, you were supposed to say something about yourself, but when it was my turn, I froze. I stared into the candle for what seemed like hours. I could not think of anything to say. Tears welled up in my eyes, but no words came to my mouth.

Around this time, my mother took me to the pediatrician and told him she thought I might be depressed. I guess he asked me a couple of questions, and then he told her I was fine. Just like that—no evaluation by a psychiatrist or therapist. Just his opinion as if it were unassailable fact. I don't remember this, but my mother told me the story when I was an adult. I wonder what help I could have gotten in the 80s anyway. It's not like emotional health was anything people talked about back then—at least, not without a whole lot of judgment.

It wasn't until I got to college that I began to fear that I had mental health issues. I heard that students could get a free counseling session, so I signed up. But once again, I couldn't find the words I needed. I sat there and cried for half an hour.

"I can't help you if you don't tell me what's wrong," the student counselor said.

I had no idea what was wrong, except for the fact that I just didn't feel right. I was always sad or angry. For thirty years, it seemed, those were the only emotions I ever experienced.

I was depressed for thirty years. I also drank for thirty years. I never put the two together until I was forty-five years old. Then it all made sense.

***

My parents drank regularly. There was a time when they drank every day. My father once claimed he had never been drunk. I doubt that, but I never saw him sloppy drunk.

My mother, it seemed, got wasted every time we went to a party. One Thanksgiving, at my Uncle Jay's house in Spring Valley, New York, Mom fell asleep in her plate before the turkey was served. That year I thanked God I was at the kids' table.

And then there was the time my neighbor got married while I was in high school. I was having fun at the reception, but then, suddenly, my dad said we had to leave. It didn't make sense. The party was still going strong, and it wasn't late at all. My dad said he wanted to go to a yarn store near the reception hall. One of his hobbies was crafting hooked rugs. But why would you leave a wedding early to go to a yarn store?

I didn't realize until years later that my dad wanted to leave because my mother was drunk. All I knew at that time was that they were bickering in the car.

"You don't know how to act at a wedding," my mom told him.

"I know what happens at weddings," he countered. "People get drunk at weddings."

At the time, I thought he was talking about people in general. I figured he just didn't like to see folks getting wasted. I thought he was an old fuddy-duddy who disliked the idea of anyone having fun.

It might have been about that time that my dad started driving to parties separately from my mom. He said he didn't want to stay out late, so he needed his own car. But as I think about it now, I wonder if there was another reason. Did he just not want to see my mom make a fool of herself? I certainly didn't. But I had also accepted that it was a part of who she was.

When I was about 12, my mother taught me to make her a gin and sour. It isn't difficult. I performed this task regularly as a child.

Drinking was normalized for me. Unlike some of my friends' families, drinking was never a taboo subject in my house. I grew up thinking that drinking was what adults did to relax.

I tried my first "real" drink when I was in the eighth grade. Oh sure, I had sipped tiny amounts of wine at the synagogue and at Passover seders. And then there were the beer bubbles I loved so much. But I'd never had a real drink until that day when I was fourteen. I opened the liquor cabinet and took out some sort of alcoholic beverage. Maybe gin. Maybe vodka. I can't remember. My parents always kept ginger ale and tonic water in the basement. The tonic water was for my mother, who sometimes liked me to fix her a gin and tonic after work. The ginger ale was for when one of us was sick. I mixed the alcoholic something-or-other with the ginger ale or tonic water, and I tried it. It wasn't very good. I drank about half of it. I felt grown up, just like I had when I drank the bubbles. I wish I had realized, at that point, that addiction runs in my family.

My mother always said that her maternal grandfather was a gambling addict. I'm pretty sure my maternal grandmother's youngest brother was an alcoholic; I never saw him without a beer in his hand. Grandma Clara's other brother got so drunk at his second wedding that he almost wasn't allowed on the plane on his way to the honeymoon. And my mom used to say the oddest thing about Grandma: "If she drank, she would have been an alcoholic."

When I was young, I thought this was silly. She didn't drink, so how would you know that? But with a gambling addict for a father and an alcoholic for a brother, it makes sense. It's probably a good thing that she didn't drink.

Perhaps the fact that addiction runs in our family is one reason my mom drank so much at parties that she embarrassed us. And perhaps it's one of the reasons I drank the way I did for so long.

***

I'm pretty sure I suffered from depression as early as high school. One year, I became a regular fixture in the school nurse's office, spending several afternoons a week there. I told myself it was a cool way of skipping class. I'd lie on the cot in the dark room for an hour or so; occasionally, I'd talk the nurse into letting me go home early. "General malaise" was always the diagnosis.

Looking back, I think I was trying to deal with my feelings the only way I could–by running away, by tuning the world out.

Later, I learned to tune the world out with liquor.

I did a lot of drinking in high school. There always seemed to be beer around, or wine coolers. They were easy to buy at the local liquor store. My friends and I would have what we called "wine and cheese" parties, which were popular with adults at the time. I'd buy some wine coolers, and we'd drink them while playing Trivial Pursuit in my kitchen when my parents worked late. My friends and I thought we were cool.

There was a song that was popular back then: "You can call me Al," by Paul Simon. Taking a cue from the song, my best friend sometimes referred to me jokingly as "Al," short for alcohol. I loved it. I didn't yet understand how negatively alcohol could affect my life.

Loneliness contributed to my drinking. I spent a lot of time by myself when I was young. I took care of myself after school from a young age, and as a teenager, I started thinking there was something different about me. I was confused about my sexuality and my gender. I knew something was going on that wasn't quite "normal," and it made me nervous. Drinking made the nervousness go away, at least for a little while.

The first time I got really drunk was in Czechoslovakia when I was touring Europe with a soccer team when I was seventeen. We had played our way through the Netherlands, France, and Germany. Now we were in a little town outside of Prague, where it seemed like the entire village came to watch us play. The hometown team demolished us. They reminded me of Amazons. I think they were all in their twenties. I noticed that they didn't shave their legs, and I found this disgusting. (Little did I know that years later I would stop shaving my legs as well.)

After the game, the home team threw us a party. There was schnapps. There was sausage. There was beer. At some point the lights went out. A Czech boy convinced me to switch shirts with him. I don't remember much else.

On the bus ride back to the hotel, I had to go to the bathroom … badly. I must have been complaining rather loudly about it, because one of my teammates produced a plastic cup. She told me to pee in the cup and then throw it out through the window at the top of the bus. This seemed like a reasonable thing to do at the time. Peeing in that cup was such a relief. I raised the cup to throw it out of the window ... and doused myself with urine.

This was one of the low points of my life, but I didn't realize it at the time.

The next day, we had another game, followed by a smaller party. I was told by several people not to drink. I didn't listen.

What began as a night of drunkenness outside Prague turned into two weeks of immaturity.

We were sleeping in a gym in Amsterdam. It was our last week in Europe, and we had just played in the Holland Cup. I remember scoring a goal in our final game. But my most prominent memory of that week is swinging from a rope in the gym, my teammates cheering me on.

"Climb that rope!" they yelled.

On the last night of the trip, I suggested to my teammates that we go out and party.

"I'm not walking you home," one girl replied.

At the time, I thought the teammate who said that was a loser. I figured I was the cool one, drinking every night. But looking back, I realize that by the end of the trip, nobody wanted to hang out with me. I guess I was the loser.

✳✳✳

We are home from college on winter break. My friends and I decide to have a party and watch Night of the Living Dead. *I have what seems like one of every drink known to humankind. The last thing I drink is Malibu rum and pineapple juice, and from that night on, I cannot stomach the stuff. Just thinking about it will give me the heebie jeebies. I wake up with the worst hangover of my life. I pour myself a bowl of Fruit Loops but can't get them down.*

My friends tell me that during the night I went into convulsions. They wanted to take me to the hospital, but I refused to go and just laughed it off.

Someone drops me off at my parents' house. There is a ton of snow on the lawn. I get out of the car and fall face-first into the snow. I somehow manage to make my way to the front door, where my mother is waiting for me.

"Hello," I say. I must reek of vomit.

"Did you throw up?"

"I don't know."

I honestly don't remember.

I crawl into bed for a few hours before I have to drive to the airport and catch a plane back to Indiana.

It is the worst airplane flight I ever have the misfortune of experiencing. I am in the front row. Remember when some planes had a front row that faced all the other rows? I have to look at all the other passengers while I try to power through a killer hangover for the entire three-and-a-half-hour flight.

***

Bloomington, Indiana. Circa 1990. I suddenly become aware that I am at a bar on Kirkwood Avenue, surrounded by fraternity brothers and sisters, and we are all drinking from the same large container, each with our own straw. "When did we get here?" I wonder. I can't remember the last few hours.

Thirty years later, I tell a friend who is in AA this story. Her response is striking:

"Non-alcoholics don't have blackouts."

***

Alcohol was not my only problem. I also experienced periodic bouts of anger. Once, in college, I slammed the closet door in my dorm room so hard that a picture fell off the wall in the next room and the frame broke. I didn't bother to apologize to the woman next door. Another time I spent several minutes throwing things across my room because I didn't get the job I wanted.

I've thrown my keys and made holes in drywall. I've screamed.

I just couldn't control my temper. I think my father had the same problem.

In the book *Alcoholics Anonymous*, which we refer to as "The Big Book," an unnamed author writes that she had failed to mature, well into adulthood: "Apparently I'd grown physically at the customary rate of speed, and I had acquired an average amount of intellectual training in the intervening years, but there had been no emotional maturity at all."[2]

Since I first read this passage about ten years ago, it has always resonated with me. I never really matured emotionally until I got sober. I was well into my 40s and still reacting like a child when things didn't go my way. It wasn't until I got sober that I was able to react less violently when something negative happened.

***

I am living in Greeley, Colorado, in the early 2000s. I am an out, single lesbian in my early thirties, eager to date. I attend the wedding of a friend from my synagogue. I meet a very pleasant older woman. We start talking. We dance. We exchange numbers. I am enamored of her. She is a grandmother and at least in her seventies. She invites me over to meet the peacock that lives in her backyard. I am desperately falling for her, but she is not interested. I am beside myself. She sings Sarah McLachlan's "Angel" to me while playing along on the accordion.

I am sobbing. She is singing my life story. What is wrong with me? I am desperate to find something. Someone. Happiness. I am so lonely. So sad. So desperately unhappy. So incredibly sick.

***

I am standing on the porch of a small house in Greeley, Colorado, some time in 2002. My friends are trying to do an intervention. I am having none of it.

"I don't have a drinking problem."

***

I'm sitting in my psychiatrist's office in Aurora, Colorado. Circa 2009.

She says I have obsessive compulsive personality disorder. That's on top of the depression and Tourette syndrome that were diagnosed years ago. Good thing I'm a hypochondriac. If I wasn't, I might be upset with all my diagnoses. But instead, I relish them.

"It's like you want to be different, but you long to fit in," the therapist says. "It's almost as if you want me to tell you there's something wrong with you."

---

2. "Alcoholics Anonymous: The Story of How Many Thousands of Men and Women Have Recovered from Alcoholism," Fourth Edition, Alcoholics Anonymous World Services, Inc., New York, 2001, page 547.

It was true. I desperately wanted to know what was wrong with me. I knew there had to be something, or else, why was I always so sad? And so angry?

My ex-wife insists that I don't have obsessive compulsive personality disorder, but according to the OCPD website, people who suffer from the syndrome have trouble expressing their emotions and are "righteous, indignant, and angry." I have all those traits. My ex says that I'm "righteous, indignant, and angry" because that's how my parents acted. She may be right. The good thing is, since getting sober, it's a lot easier for me to express my feelings, and I'm not nearly as "righteous, indignant, and angry" as I once was.

I don't know if I have OCPD, but I do have some OCD symptoms. For instance, I often fear that something terrible is going to happen to my biceps–like maybe they will rupture–so I have to run my hands over them slowly again and again. It's the oddest feeling. I know intellectually that nothing is going to happen to my biceps, but that feeling still seems to overwhelm me every once in a while.

I definitely have Tourette's. I discovered this in my early twenties, when I started making woofing sounds for seemingly no reason. My parents had recently told me about their impending divorce, and I had gone into a deep depression. I lost weight and started seeing a therapist, who prescribed the antidepressant Zoloft. I thought at first that the medicine had brought on the woofing, so I asked my therapist to prescribe something else. I went on Paxil, another antidepressant, and have been on it ever since. But the woofing persisted.

I saw a physician at Yale who studied Tourette's, and he diagnosed me the disease. And while it started with woofs, I have other tics as well. Sometimes I meow. Sometimes I say offensive things. For a while I would say, "Dogs are comin' over." Rarely, I say, "Suck it, bitch." I usually only say these things when I'm alone or in a safe environment, like with family or close friends.

Although I first noticed the tics in my twenties, I believe my Tourette's began presenting itself much earlier. My mother once reminded me that I used to put my hand to my nose and sniff loudly when I was a teen, over and over. I would do this with my right hand and then my left. This is called "evening up" and is often seen in people with OCD as well as Tourette's. For instance, if I touch my right leg by accident, I often feel the need to touch my left leg in the same way. If I don't do it exactly right, I need to repeatedly touch both legs until I feel it's "perfect."

When I was in my early forties, my psychiatrist prescribed a very low dose of a medication that controls the Tourette's (for the most part) while also stabilizing my mood. I still experience tics, but not as often. I am thankful for this.

Many people misunderstand the disease because they have a cartoon concept of it. I think the depiction of Tourette's in movies and TV shows is one reason people don't understand it. It's much funnier and weirder when people swear uncontrollably than when they say things like "woof" and "meow." When I have told people about it in the past, they often dismissed me, saying that I couldn't have it because I wasn't swearing non-stop. I even had a therapist in graduate school who told me I didn't have it. I immediately walked out of her office and never returned.

My father once told me that he asked his doctor about it and was told that he, too, had Tourette's. I know he compulsively picked at the hair on his face, but I didn't notice any verbal tics. I guess it's something else I should have asked him about when I had the chance.

***

"You know, you shouldn't drink on that medicine," my mother warned. Many times.

She was right. The label on my antidepressants clearly read "Do NOT drink alcohol while taking this medication."

Why did I not follow that advice? Because I simply could not NOT drink. It was an obsession.

I'd drink with absolutely no intention of drinking. It was like there was a phantom power lurking over me. And drinking counteracted the medicine.

Alcohol is a depressant. Plain and simple.

***

My son and I are visiting my mother in Durham, North Carolina. We are planning brunch at a fancy French restaurant. I call to make a reservation.

"What time would you like to come in?" the host asks.

"What time do you start serving alcohol?"

"Noon."

"Noon it is."

My mother laughs.

***

I'm emptying the dishwasher in my kitchen in Lakewood, Colorado. I am in my early forties.

"There's something wrong with me."

I am blubbering.

My partner tells me to stop it.

I don't know what's wrong with me. But I do so want to know. I feel lost. Unmoored.

A few years later, I have this crazy idea that I will go to law school at night in South Denver while teaching in Greeley, two hours to the north, during the day—even though I have no desire to be a lawyer. I start studying for the LSAT. I suppose I just want to prove that I am smart enough to get through law school. It's like when I was in my early twenties and wanted to go to rabbinical school. I didn't want to be a rabbi. I just wanted something new to occupy my life because my current situation was so awful.

***

One of the problems, which I would find out a few years later, was alcohol. The other problem was that I spent almost eight years in a very unhealthy relationship. I had low self-esteem. I didn't know what a healthy relationship was. My parents weren't good role models in that department. My partner and I yelled at each other a lot, but I thought that was normal. We weren't right for each other, and maybe we tried to make it work for too long. It was hard to end the relationship, but I'm glad now that Darrian had two parents who were happy for much of his childhood. I don't know if that would have been the case if we'd stayed together.

***

Once my partner and I broke up, I had a lot of time to myself.

I drank alone at night, after I put my son to bed.

I drank Jack Daniel's. A lot of Jack Daniel's.

One day I opened my mail and looked at my credit card statement. There was a charge for a dating site I didn't remember signing up for. Had I joined the site while I was drunk? That's the only explanation I could think of.

My solution was to stop buying Jack Daniel's. I drank beer instead. A lot of beer. Then I stopped buying beer and only drank when I was away from home. Once I joined AA, I learned that these are classic alcoholic moves.

A few months before I decided to get sober, a good friend stopped drinking and smoking weed. My response to this was telling: "I guess we can't hang out anymore."

"Why not?"

"Well, if we can't drink…"

Again, this was alcoholic thinking. The way we "hung out" was to sit around, drink beer and talk. Why couldn't we sit around and talk without beer?

***

Every alcoholic eventually reaches a bottom—the low point at which there is nowhere to go but up, when they realize it's time to do something. My bottom came at a birthday party for an acquaintance in the Capitol Hill section of Denver when I was forty-five. The birthday girl had purchased a large bottle of Jameson Irish Whiskey for her friends to share. Being a Jack Daniel's fan, I wasn't thrilled at the beginning of the evening, but I proceeded to drink six glasses of the stuff.

At the end of the night, as I walked the three blocks to my car, I pondered eating breakfast at one of my favorite spots, Pete's Kitchen, a greasy spoon not far from where I once lived. But I decided against it.

The next day, I woke up at home, but I didn't remember driving. For the first time in my life I thought I might have a problem with alcohol. I had driven drunk many, many times. But for some reason, this time it hit differently.

I called my therapist.

"Try to quit for two weeks," she said. "If you can't, you might have a problem."

I lasted twelve days.

It was Thanksgiving. I had invited a friend over. I could have a little wine with dinner, couldn't I? Then we went out to play poker, and I proceeded to drink several beers.

I called a good friend who had been sober for a few years. I hemmed and hawed, trying to decide if there was really a problem or if I was just making a big deal out of nothing. My friend gave it to me straight: "Non-alcoholics don't wonder if they're alcoholics."

I heard something similar at an AA meeting when I was a few months sober.

"You know," a woman said, "I don't sit around asking myself if I'm allergic to strawberries."

Of course she wasn't allergic to strawberries. That's why she never wondered about it. Yet before they get sober, alcoholics are always asking themselves if they really have a problem. If you're allergic to strawberries, you know it. It's the same with alcohol. It's just that people don't want to admit they have a problem with booze.

***

I worked with nine therapists over a quarter of a century. I suppose that's no record, but it certainly wasn't a small investment of my life. I'm just estimating here, but let's say I attended two counseling sessions a month. At $20 a pop for the co-pay, that's $480 a year. Over 25 years, that's $12,000. I'm sure I learned something important about myself during all those sessions, but I'm not sure it was worth that much money.

None of those therapists ever gave me what I needed because I never admitted what the real problem was. Since getting sober in 2013, I have experienced few symptoms of depression. And I feel feelings other than anger and sadness. And when I do feel my feelings, I am able to deal with them maturely, for the most part. I'm also finally able to work with a therapist and really get at the issues that matter.

I've learned in AA that many alcoholics drink because we don't want to feel our feelings. When I was young, I wasn't allowed to show my emotions. If I cried or looked upset, my father would yell at me. Neither of my parents dealt very well with emotions, so I had no role model to look to about this. I pushed my feelings down and became depressed. And when I discovered alcohol, I learned that drinking covered up the emotions, so I didn't have to feel them. Alcohol also helped cover up the feelings I was having about being attracted to women. And about how I didn't quite fit in my female body. And to counter my low self-esteem. It was so much easier to talk to people—to just feel "normal"—with a beer in my hand.

It's so much better in sobriety.

I'm down from sixty milligrams a day of my antidepressant to twenty. I'll probably always suffer from a bit of depression, but I feel better than I have in my adult life. From the time I was fifteen to the time I was forty-five, I was never truly happy. I never imagined I could experience joy like I feel now. And most of all, I'm at peace.

***

The truth is that for thirty years I was obsessed with alcohol. I thought about it all the time. I craved it. And once I tasted it, I craved more. According to the Big Book, alcoholism is like an allergy. When alcoholics drink, they crave more. No one knows why this happens.

I was lucky that I had a very high bottom, but it probably kept me from seeking help much sooner.

When I began attending AA meetings, I wasn't sure if I fit in. I heard people talking about rehab, DUIs, losing everything. Nothing like that had happened to me … yet.

Someone told me to look for the similarities, not the differences. And I began to see that I was just as sick as any of the people who had ended up in detox or lost their jobs because of alcohol.

At my low point, I didn't see any hope. Every night, as my head hit the pillow, I would say to myself, "God, I hate my life. I wanna die."

If that's not hitting bottom, I don't know what is.

Alcoholism is a disease of the body, mind, and spirit.

My spirit had been broken. My mind was filled with anger and sadness. My body was still functioning pretty well, but how long would that last?

I went to meetings. I worked with a sponsor. I read the Big Book. And I worked the Twelve Steps. That's how I got well. And today, instead of thinking about dying every night, I can't wait to go to sleep so I can get up and do it all over the next day. Talk about a 180-degree turn.

***

My mother died when I was barely two months sober. It could have been a disaster, yet I never felt like drinking.

"You're so calm," my brother remarked about an hour after she died.

"I haven't had a drink in 70 days," I answered.

He had expected me to act like I always had, cursing and screaming in a rage. But I had put my faith in a higher power, and I didn't need to act like that anymore.

My mother's best friend brought us food the next day, and she also brought a bottle of wine and a six pack of beer. I didn't even think about indulging. I didn't need to. God had me. And I had God.

One of the requirements of the Twelve Steps is belief in a higher power, not necessarily God. Many people drop out because they either never believed in God or feel conflicted about the God of their childhoods. I never had this problem. I have always had a profound belief in God. But before I got sober, I didn't really have a relationship with God. I went to synagogue and said the prayers on Fridays and Saturdays and holidays, but I never asked God for help. That wasn't even something I would have thought of before. After I started working the AA program, I realized that God was there for me all the time, not just when I was in the synagogue or at the Seder table.

Before I got sober, I used to lie in bed and imagine scenarios in which the woman I was pining for would love me. Now I understand that God has me, and I don't need to worry about making all my wishes come true.

I heard it said once that God answers all prayers, but sometimes the answer is "no." I know that God has a plan for me, even when it involves some "nos." And that gives me comfort.

***

When I became an assistant professor in 2000, I knew I had to publish my research to get tenure and a promotion. But at that time, I was too busy playing soccer and partying to publish. After seven years at my university, I only had one article, and it didn't appear in a juried publication. I guess it was no surprise that I was denied tenure. I made a rash decision; instead of looking for another tenure-track job, I opted to stay and teach four classes instead of three and give up research. I prefer teaching to research, but this decision made it nearly impossible for me to ever get a full-time teaching job at another university.

I stayed on as an assistant professor for the next seven years, and I pretty much hated every minute of it. I hated my job. I hated the dean who'd denied me tenure. I didn't hate my colleagues or my students, but I'm not sure I treated them all that well.

Once I sobered up and started working the Twelve Steps, things changed. I took myself and my work more seriously. I started dressing up for work in a dress shirt and tie. It felt nice to see my exterior match my interior a bit more. In a way, getting sober allowed me to finally start becoming myself.

I remember working on Step Nine, which involves making amends to the people you've hurt. One by one, I met with each of the other faculty members in my department and told them I wasn't drinking anymore and that I would try to be a better colleague. And the strangest thing happened. I began to enjoy my job. I began to like my colleagues again. And I began to respect my students and treat them with compassion. About a year after I made those amends, I finally got my promotion to associate professor. I still don't have tenure, so I don't have the job security that I would have had if I'd done what I was supposed to do to begin with, but I love my job. Today, after 24 years, I am finally a full professor. I love teaching students to write and edit because I love to write and edit. I love seeing them progress from youngsters with some talent to adults who are ready to work as professional journalists.

***

I wasn't someone who passed out every time I drank. I didn't drink every night. But it wasn't about how much I drank or how often. It was about why I drank and what it did to me.

I drank when I didn't want to. I drank alone. I'd grow impatient with my son until he finally went to sleep so I could pour the Jack Daniel's or crack open a beer.

"I shouldn't be doing this," I'd say to myself as I opened another one.

On the ride to Denver to meet friends, I'd tell myself that I was only going out to dance. I wouldn't drink.

"Jack Daniel's on the rocks," I'd tell the bartender as soon as I got there.

I even drank the night before I was planning to go to my first AA meeting. I had a few glasses of Jameson and decided to call it a night. Then one of my friends offered to buy me a drink. So I stayed and drank more.

This is what you call insanity.

I don't think my father understood how AA worked, and I don't think he thought I was an alcoholic.

"You still going to AA?" He would ask this every time I saw him.

"Yes. I need to go for the rest of my life."

He would give me a look of incredulity. I think maybe he was under the impression that all alcoholics lived on the street or under bridges.

One thing I've learned in AA is that no one can label you an alcoholic but yourself. I once read that an alcoholic is anyone whose life gets better when they stop drinking. That's definitely true for me.

***

I never fit in when I was a kid. I never fit in as an adult. When I got to AA, I found my people. It was like coming home.

A couple of years ago, I got my second tattoo: a peace symbol with the words "serenity, courage, wisdom" on the inside of my lower left arm. It's an abbreviated version of the Serenity Prayer, which opens most AA meetings: "God, grant me the serenity to accept the things I cannot change, courage to change the things I can, and the wisdom to know the difference." This prayer has guided me through my sober life, and I hope to keep saying it for the rest of my days.

More importantly, because I put the AA program into my life, I now have a serenity that I never had before. Unlike during the first forty-five years of my life, I don't yell and scream and kick things when I don't get my way. I have the strength to get through difficult times. I have the courage to do things I never thought I could do, like deal with the deaths of my parents and a cancer diagnosis. And I have the wisdom to know that some things are out of my control. I can't make people act a certain way, no matter how hard I try. I can't make my students study and work hard. And that's okay.

When I got the tattoo, a friend who is also in the AA program went with me. I told the tattoo artist what I wanted, and he made a temporary tat of it in the back room. I noticed that the words were in the wrong order. He looked at the temporary tattoo and did a double take. I could see he was saying the Serenity Prayer to himself. He told us later that he was a heroin addict but was in recovery. He knew the prayer well. At that moment, I realized it was meant to be. Not just the tattoo, but the life I was living. With sobriety as my foundation, everything else made sense.

Living this way is simple, but it's not easy. Having the tattoo on the inside of my arm, where I can see it, serves as a reminder every day of how I want to live my life. It reminds me that I have found serenity, courage, and wisdom.

***

Why was I so obsessed with alcohol?

I drank because I didn't want to feel my feelings—feelings of inadequacy, gender confusion, attraction to women. I covered up those feelings, and I created a feminine persona so I could fit in. The more I pushed down those emotions, the more I had to drink to numb the pain.

After getting sober, I was able to have a fulfilling relationship for the first time in my life. I married someone who respected me and treated me with kindness. It didn't work out, but it showed me what a healthy relationship looks like and gave me hope that I can have an even better relationship in the future.

Another truth about my relationship with my ex-wife is that it would never have been possible had I not gotten sober. She indicated on her online profile that she rarely drank. I would never have looked twice at her in my drinking days after reading that. But it's much more than that. It's the fact that I was just not ready to be a good partner while I was drinking. I didn't know who I was; I couldn't even accept myself. So I was in no position to really love and accept someone else.

I know that getting sober is the most important thing I ever did. It allowed me to have all the wonderful things I have today: a strong relationship with my son, friends I can count on, a job I love. And I have found a new partner. It's the healthiest relationship I've ever had. I still have trouble sharing my emotions sometimes, but I'm getting better at it.

I heard something a long time ago in an AA meeting, and it still rings true for me today: AA helped me become the person I was meant to be.

Maybe most importantly, getting sober led me to embrace my true self.

With my parents the day I was awarded my doctorate.

6

Call me Eli

It was the first day of Hebrew class my freshman year at Indiana University. The teacher went around asking each of us our names, *in Hebrew*. Hebrew is a gendered language. Many words that are gender-neutral in English are either masculine or feminine in Hebrew. That makes someone like me an anomaly.

Even the question of "what's your name" is gendered. For a man, it's pronounced something like "*ma shimcha*?" For a woman, it's more like "*ma shimach*?" When the teacher got to me, she stumbled.

"… *Ma … shimach*?" she said, hoping she'd guessed right. She had.

Many of us used our Hebrew names in the class. It's customary to give a Jewish child a Hebrew name as well as an English name. The Hebrew name is used to call someone to the Torah, our holy book, during services. I think my parents chose "Elisha" because the first consonant is an L, just like in my given name, Lynn.

And when the teacher asked my name that day in class, I was proud to reply.

"Elisha," I said.

The teacher looked at me a little funny.

"But this is a boy's name," she said.

"Well, it's my name," I answered, feeling the blood rushing to my face.

I learned recently that "Elisha" is a gender-neutral name, which suits me just fine. But back then, as a young woman who didn't quite look like a young woman, and didn't quite feel like a young woman, and didn't quite act like a young woman (whatever that meant) my experience that day in Hebrew class was devastating.

***

During the Jewish holiday of Purim, people dress up in costumes and try to get so drunk that they can't tell the difference between the phrases "Blessed is Mordechai" and "Cursed is Haman." When I was very young, I played Mordechai in our Sunday school play. Mordechai is a male relative of Queen Esther, the heroine of the story. It wasn't a big deal back then that I played a man in the skit. Purim is about blurring the lines. Between good and evil. Between masculine and feminine. A rabbi once said that we are all the evil Haman, we are all Mordechai, we are all Esther, and we must embrace all those parts. This makes sense when it comes to gender. In the Jewish tradition, God has both masculine and feminine attributes. And if we're created *B'tzelem Elohim*—in God's image—we must all have both male and female inside us. It's up to us to embrace all of that. I have been doing this all my life.

***

Kids look me up and down, trying to figure me out. And unlike adults, children aren't held back by tact. They need to know.

When I was in graduate school, I became friendly with two of my classmates who were married. The youngest of their three children, who was about six, once asked me, "Are you a boy or a girl?" I was so embarrassed I could say nothing but "Ask your mother." I was frustrated with myself afterward because I'd had a chance to tell her that girls don't have to look a certain way. I missed that chance because of my shame … or maybe because, at the time, I couldn't accept myself.

***

When I was in kindergarten, all my friends were boys. My best friend, David, lived across the street from me. I remember playing with David and another boy, Ricky, one day. Ricky was a bit younger than David and I.

"Let's play house," Ricky suggested.

"That's girly stuff," I said.

House? Give me a break. I wanted to play baseball or kickball or football. Anything but house. I just never took a shine to girly stuff. And it showed.

I was a funny-looking little kid. I wore glasses, and I was so thin that other kids sometimes called me "Skinny Lynnie." I had rather prominent buck teeth.

I rarely wore dresses. I preferred jeans, T-shirts, and baseball caps. I also wore my hair very short, something not many girls did in the 1970s and early '80s.

As a result of all this, I was often mistaken for a boy.

I remember once raising my hand to answer a question, and the substitute teacher called on me. "That boy in the striped shirt," she said. Everyone laughed. "That's a girl," they shouted. It wasn't funny to me. I was embarrassed. I wanted to fit in, but I certainly didn't want to dress like a girl.

One time in elementary school, I wore a dress for picture day. I arrived early and waited for the other students. Just as I was beginning to feel like I could pull it off, one of my classmates arrived.

"You look better in pants," she said.

If I had not already been convinced that I wasn't a real girl, this comment cemented it. If I had been a real girl, she might have said something like, "You look nice today."

***

I started making people uncomfortable with my gender bending when I was very young.

I was walking home from school with a bunch of friends, bound for a party. An older boy yelled across the street, "Hey, is that a boy or a girl?"

"She's a girl," all my friends shouted back. They were used to my gender-bending. Although they may not have understood me, they accepted me.

But this older boy did not.

"Take down your pants and prove it!" he yelled.

Everyone laughed, but I was devastated. I don't remember crying on the outside, but I'm sure I was dying on the inside. Even at that point, so young and innocent, not yet aware of puberty, I felt there was something wrong with me. I didn't fit in. I wasn't a real girl.

It got worse in high school. It seemed like every time I opened my mouth in class, the boys would laugh at me. I wonder now why the teachers never did anything about this.

Once I wrote my name on a desk in English class. (Pretty stupid, I know.) When I got to class the next day, someone had changed it to read "Lynn Silverstein … is a fucking guy. She wears a cup and jockstrap."

More evidence that I wasn't a real girl. And more shame about who I really was.

Maybe I felt shame because I never felt right being a girl, and in some ways, I guess I wanted to be a boy.

My locker was plastered with photos of the football player Doug Flutie. On my bedroom wall hung a giant poster of James Dean in a red leather jacket. Back then, I thought I was attracted to these men. Now I think I wanted to be these men. I wanted their bravado. Their machismo. Their very essence of maleness.

***

According to Jamison Green, who writes about this issue in his ground-breaking book, *Becoming a Visible Man*, I had a "transgender childhood," which Green defines as one in which a child blends the genders in a way that many people aren't sure what to do with. Other people were uncomfortable with my gender, so I was uncomfortable with it. Yet looking back, my gender bending was only uncomfortable for me when other people called attention to it. This was the case for most of my life, even in adulthood.

I remember car shopping with my mother outside Athens, Ohio, when I was about 30. My mom was chatting with the salesman.

"Is this your son?"

I was perfectly okay with this mistaken identity. Then my mom corrected him. "It's my daughter."

It was only at this point that I was completely embarrassed.

When people didn't correct themselves, it felt good. Once I went to the grocery store, and the cashier referred to me as "sir" three times. I came home happy.

***

Once, as an adult, I asked my mom, "Why didn't you make me wear a dress once in a while?"

"We tried," she said. "For your brother's Bar Mitzvah."

The day my brother became a man, I wore an orange and cream pants suit. I also wore a kippah, the skullcap that men and boys wore at that time in some synagogues. (Today many women and nonbinary people wear them as well.) I felt so proud of my seven-year-old self. Everyone accepted me. I felt like *myself*. It was a big day for our family. Some parents would have forced their daughter to wear a dress. It was the 1970s, for goodness' sake. Most people knew nothing about gender being a continuum. Looking back, I realize my mom and dad accepted me when many people didn't. Thank God for them.

Yet when I became a Bat Mitzvah at fourteen, I wore a dress. It was 1982. What choice did I have? I felt totally out of place that day. Don't get me wrong. It was a wonderful day for me. I was proud. I got to have all my friends there with me to celebrate. Yet there was something missing.

A week after my son became a Bar Mitzvah a few years ago, we attended the Bat Mitzvah of a girl in his class. She wore combat boots and a tie. I happened to be wearing a tie that day as well. I told her how great she looked. I couldn't help but feel a pang of envy. She had the guts to do what I could only have dreamed of back in 1982. Of course, I doubt I would have even thought to wear a tie to my Bat Mitzvah. But, wow, would I have loved that. It would have made the perfect day for me.

I'm glad so many kids today are more comfortable in their own skin than I ever was as a child. We've definitely progressed as a society. But there is still lots of work to be done. There are many places, and many families, where children are not allowed to be who they are.

I was accepted as a child, even if I didn't really accept myself. I tried desperately to fit in. I always felt like a laughingstock because I was a tomboy. It wasn't until I went to graduate school, joined Swarm of Dykes, and minored in women's studies that (ironically) I began to *accept* my masculine side. It wasn't until my mid-forties that I *embraced* that side of me. It wasn't until my mid-fifties that I truly *found* myself.

***

I just never could pull off that femme stuff. As a kid, If I wore a nice pair of pants, I'd end up with grass stains on them by the end of the day. I couldn't walk in fancy shoes. Yet I continued to try to blend in.

I served as a bridesmaid at my brother's wedding when I was nineteen. I was totally out of my element. When my then-fiancée saw a photo album of the event years later, with me wearing a pink dress and a matching comb in my hair, she was aghast. I had a stunned look on my face in every shot. I probably would have been more comfortable as an usher, wearing a tuxedo.

Twenty-five years later, my brother got married for a second time. It was a much smaller affair—no bridesmaids or ushers. I wore a suit. It was a woman's suit, an Ann Taylor piece, but it was a far cry from his first wedding.

"I'm sure it will look beautiful on you," my friend told me when she saw a picture of the suit.

"I prefer to be called handsome," was my response.

The night before the wedding, both immediate families dined together. Introducing myself to my future sister-in-law's brother, I got a bit tongue-tied. I meant to say "I'm Lynn. Geoff's my brother," but something else came out.

"I'm Lynn, Geoff's ... brother," I stammered.

Never one to pass up a joke, my mother immediately replied, "You wish."

I was a bit embarrassed, but not much. I realized maybe she was right. And I didn't feel ashamed like when I was young. I had grown into my gender.

***

I used to attend a weekly all-women AA meeting. Once, I was sitting in the meeting with about fifty other people. I had come directly from work, so I was wearing a boy's dress shirt and a tie. My hair was quite short. A woman who hadn't been to the meeting before sat down beside me.

"I thought it would be all women," she said to me.

"It is all women," I answered.

"You're a woman?" she asked, seemingly stunned.

Even though I'm only five foot five, I have been mistaken for a man many times. I've always felt more comfortable in traditionally male-coded clothing.

Speaking of which, why are some clothes labeled "male" and some "female"? Why do stores have separate departments for women and men's clothing, or boys and girls? Why do we care about what other people wear?

And make no mistake about it. We do care. Very much. It's almost as if people need to know what sex you are the moment they see you. What is that about? Are our primitive brains trying to figure out whether someone would make a good mate?

Even infants are gendered from the moment they're born, and sometimes even before that. It used to be that the first question people would ask when a baby was born was, "Is it a boy or a girl?" Today, expectant parents throw gender reveal parties while the fetus is still in-utero. We enter the gender binary before birth. And woe to those who rock the gender boat.

Jamison Green says that many people are threatened by those who don't fit the gender binary, and they often react with anger.

I agree that many people are threatened by those who don't fit the gender norms. But I often feel like I'm the one being threatened. Maybe I'm threatened by myself because I still feel shame around who I am. It's like I still want to fit in, to be a real girl. But I just don't feel like one. Sometimes I don't feel like a woman *or* a man. It's like I'm right in the middle. Of course, psychologists have been talking about gender as a continuum for years. Yet sometimes the situation still makes me feel like an anomaly.

***

During graduate school, around the same time I joined Swarm of Dykes, I got a crew cut. This was also the first time I'd ever heard the term "transgender," as there were a few trans men in the group.

Sporting my crew cut in Southeastern Ohio, in the middle of Appalachia, I did tend to make people uncomfortable. I didn't wear earrings or make up. (Still don't.) Women often looked askance at me when I entered the ladies' room. To this day, I feel weird in the women's bathroom. I'm always afraid someone will see me and be taken aback, mistake me for a man, attack me for being there.

I experience that fear a lot. When I used to use the locker room at the gym, I wondered what I'd say to someone who mistook me for a man. It happened a couple of times, but I never responded. I mostly just tried to laugh it off. But I've come up with some great comebacks over the years:

• "Not all women look alike. Thank God."

• "Do you think I'm so ridiculously stupid that I don't know which locker room to use? Idiot."

I'm always on alert.

When I used to enter the restroom, I would stand a little straighter so that my breasts appeared more prominent, but now that I wear a breast binder, I can't do that. I just try to get in and out as fast as I can and hope no one sees me.

When state legislatures started enacting "bathroom bills" a few years ago, I was worried. There were a few incidents in which "masculine-looking" women were thrown out of restrooms.

I don't really understand all the fuss about transgender people using the bathroom in which they feel comfortable. The women's room has stalls, after all. It's not like anyone sees anyone else with her pants down. Girls and women are not in danger because of trans women using the ladies' room. The people who are really in danger are transgender men and women. If a transphobic man, or any man who is insecure about his sexuality, found out a trans man was using the men's bathroom, he might attack that person. And can you imagine what would happen if a trans woman were to enter the men's room because her birth certificate labeled her male? That's a scary situation to contemplate, and one that might end with a trans woman being attacked.

I don't pretend to speak for transgender people. I'm more gender queer, or nonbinary. I float somewhere between male and female. I just don't fit the neat little boxes society has created for us.

I understand that "bathroom bills" are all about fear and society's latent queerphobia. Yet for me, it's almost as though straight people are now beginning to feel the awkwardness I've always felt. And maybe that's good. Maybe it will help them appreciate—just a little bit—what it's like for folks who don't fit the gender binary.

I used to avoid the restroom at work during busy times. I just didn't feel comfortable standing in line—like I was on display. I felt as if I didn't belong.

A few years ago, I met with the dean to talk about changing one of the bathrooms in our building to all-gender. About a year later, that idea came to fruition. That felt good because not only was it one less thing for me to worry about, but I felt like I helped bring about a change that will make gender non-conforming students feel more comfortable, too. In some ways, maybe I consider it a gift to my younger self.

But still, when I'm out in public, I seek out family restrooms, just to be safe. And if I'm going out somewhere in a more conservative area, I make sure to go to the restroom before I leave. That way, I don't have to worry. But sometimes you just have to go, and more often than not, there's no family restroom. At those times, I always have to steel myself before seeking out the ladies' room. It's something I'll probably have to deal with for the rest of my life. And it's far from easy. The only way around this problem is dressing and grooming in a more "feminine" way, and that's not something I'm willing to do.

Even though I now embrace myself, for the most part, I still cringe a little when I have to use a restroom that's intended for women only. Recently, however, I tried the men's room for the first time. It was thrilling, but a bit scary.

I recently spent a few hours at the public library in Boulder, Colorado. The main floor has one bathroom. Each stall has its own door. Everyone uses this bathroom. No one makes a big deal about it. I wish every building were like this, and that every community was so welcoming.

***

When I was very little, my father got my older brother a plastic razor so he could pretend to shave. I was jealous of being left out, so my dad got me a razor, too. My plastic razor was red. I remember lathering my face with shaving cream and pretending to shave in front of the bathroom mirror. I felt proud, like I was all grown up. I didn't know it then, but that act of pretend shaving was a sign of things to come.

When I was in high school, my mother took me to her gynecologist. She was worried because I had so much thick, dark hair all over my body. Looking back, I can't understand why she thought this was a problem. Her concern certainly made me think there was something wrong with me. Once again, I wasn't female enough. I wasn't a real girl. The interesting thing was that my mom had the very same problem with her body hair. Did she think there was something wrong with her, as well? Incidentally, the men in my family also have a lot of thick, dark body hair. My brother was once mistaken for a Bear (a big, hairy, gay man) when he accompanied me to the Pride parade in Denver—a fact that he laughingly reminds me of on occasion.

So I went to the gynecologist. After a very painful pelvic exam, the doctor told me he couldn't find anything wrong with me, so he sent me to an endocrinologist. Another very painful exam followed. That doctor actually had the audacity to say, during the exam, while I was screaming in pain, "I thought the other doctor opened you up." Afterward, I told my mother how awful it was. She did not offer any words of consolation. Instead, she told me to get used to it. I cried again. (To this day, I take Valium before a pelvic exam just to get through it.)

The endocrinologist told me I had something called "adrenal hyperplasia." He said my adrenal gland was making "too much of a certain hormone." He wouldn't tell me exactly which hormone it was, so I assumed it was the "male" hormone. Why didn't he tell me which hormone it was? Did he think I was going to kill myself because I had too much "male" hormone running rampant through my veins?

I don't really understand the fuss about "male" and "female" hormones. How do the so-called experts decide what amount of "male" hormone is "too much" for a woman to have? What amount of "male" hormone makes a woman "abnormal"? And why are they even referred to as "male" and "female"? If women have them, how can they be "male"?

The doctor gave me some pills, and I took them for a few years. I don't remember them doing anything at all about the excessive hair growth. I stopped taking them when I was in my mid-twenties because, by that point, I no longer cared about which hormones were coursing through my veins. But for a long time, I fixated on the fact that I was somehow not a real woman because of my "hormone problem." I have come to understand that the amount of a certain hormone in one's veins doesn't make one male or female and that too much of one hormone doesn't make one "abnormal."

But the problem of excessive hair growth continued to haunt me for years. I began getting electrolysis in college and continued the process on and off until I was in my mid-thirties. I guess it was one more way I tried to fit in. But despite all the treatments, the hair on my face continued to be a problem. I even tried laser treatments in my forties. But the hair kept coming back.

One day I decided to start shaving. It worked. It was the first time in my adult life I could get through the day without feeling self-conscious about my facial hair. Today I shave pretty much every day. I think shaving lets me get in touch with that masculine part of myself that I denied for so many years. It's something I've come to love.

Occasionally, I let my "beard" grow out for a couple of days, and I really like that. Once, I let it go for a week. It looked awful, but I enjoyed having that scruff on my chin. I couldn't help but rub it every few minutes. (Now I know why men do that.) I sometimes wish I had the courage to let it grow for good. I would love to just let go and see what it's like to pass as a man out there in the world. It's scary, but also exciting.

Despite the epiphany of shaving (and sometimes not shaving), I was still haunted by hormones. I had a genetic test done when I was in my late forties and found out I was 100 percent female—a fact that didn't surprise me but disappointed me a little. Looking back, I've tried to figure out what was going on in my mind that made me want to get tested in the first place. I had always had regular periods. Why did I think I might not be female? Maybe it was the bullying I endured when I was young that left me scarred. Maybe it was the hormone imbalance. Maybe it was internalized homophobia. Maybe it was the fact that I never really felt "right" in my female body. Maybe I secretly wanted to be male.

***

In grad school, I hunted in thrift stores for used men's clothing. I began wearing boy's dress shirts and ties to teach my classes. I stopped shaving my legs and my underarms. I wanted to be the most in-your-face dyke I could be.

I was so convincingly masculine that at a journalism conference in Washington, D.C., U.S. Rep. Barney Frank mistook me for a man when I asked him a question during a Q and A, though he corrected himself right away. My mother saw this on C-SPAN and laughed hysterically.

Around this same time, I attended a family party on the East Coast to celebrate my aunt and uncle's twenty-fifth wedding anniversary. I didn't realize it was going to be a fancy affair, so all I had brought with me were jeans, a cable sweater, and combat boots. My relatives didn't know what to make of me, what with my crew cut and all.

When I got to Colorado a few years later, I was still pretty in-your-face for a few years. But then my therapist told me not to be "so hard." Maybe she thought being softer would help cure my anger problem. I shaved my legs and my armpits. I got rid of the black leather motorcycle jacket that I loved and started wearing a lot of pink. I met a woman, and we fell in love. She liked to buy me clothes at the thrift store. Sometimes these clothes were more feminine than I preferred.

Around this time, I went to another fancy family party back East, and I wore a dress my grandmother had made. My mother's sister, who was in her seventies at the time, commented that my partner was having a positive influence on me.

"You see? You don't have to wear combat boots," she said.

But no matter what my aunt may have thought, wearing a dress was just not me.

After I got sober when I was forty-five, I went back to wearing ties. I bought boys' shirts and men's jeans to hang out in. I stopped shaving my legs for good. I found out that men's underwear is really comfortable. And I bought another motorcycle jacket, which I love. A few years later, I stopped shaving my underarms, too.

About a month after I met the woman who would become my wife, she sent me a photo of herself wearing her prom dress. I asked her to bring the dress over so we could have our own prom. I made a mixtape of music I thought she'd enjoy. I wore a dress shirt, tie, and vest. We danced for about forty-five minutes, until the music stopped. It was the prom I never had. Of course, I went to prom in high school, but I never really *went to prom*. Not like this, with a beautiful woman as my date and a tie around my neck. It was who I was supposed to be. It felt so right.

On the day we got married, we both wore ties.

Does this affinity for "male" clothing mean I'm transgender? Maybe.

I recently started taking testosterone, but I'm microdosing, so the physical changes won't start for about seven months. But eventually, my voice will deepen, my body hair will become more pronounced, and my muscle structure will change. It makes me giddy just thinking about it.

But am I male? Can I be nonbinary and take testosterone at the same time? I am the only one who gets to make that decision. And for now, I guess I'm still nonbinary. I may change my mind in a few months, a few years, or a decade from now. And I am OK with that.

In some ways, I do enjoy embracing my feminine side as well as my masculine side. I love pedicures. My favorite color is pink. I know nail polish and pink aren't just for women, but they do add an interesting element to my gender blend. And "I am Woman" is still one of my all-time favorite songs.

But I also really like Brad Paisley's "I'm Still a Guy," and I always sing along when this song comes on. Once, back in high school, I was in the locker room changing for gym class, and I was singing "You Really Got Me" by the Kinks. It's a song about a guy lusting for a gal.

My friend scolded me. "Lynn, can't you sing a song that a woman would sing?"

I was taken aback. I had never thought to sing a song that a woman would sing.

I guess not much has changed. But back then I was embarrassed. Today, I take pride in my ability to straddle the divide between the masculine and the feminine.

My gender bending still causes me consternation sometimes, though. When I appeared on *Jeopardy!* in a necktie, some internet trolls must have said some nasty things, because one of my opponents contacted me after our show ran to apologize for "what they were saying" on Twitter. I also received an email from a complete stranger who wrote that she was glad I lost my second game because "women should dress and act like women." A few years later, my teenage son told me there was an internet thread about me connected with the show. I made the mistake of looking it up. I only read one comment: "Lynn hasn't chosen a gender yet."

I'm still not sure why people I've never met are so concerned with what's in my pants.

***

Judith Butler argues in her book *Gender Trouble* that gender, like sexuality, is not an essential truth obtained from one's body but something that is acted out and portrayed as "reality." Am I portraying the male gender when I don a tie? Was I performing the female gender when I wore a pink gown to my high school prom? Don't we all portray a gender each day when we leave the house dressed in whatever we feel comfortable wearing?

I was listening to a radio program about transgender people a few years ago and heard something that struck a chord. Someone said that a trans woman has "the soul of a woman in the body of a man." I thought to myself, "maybe I have the soul of a man in the body of a woman."

Looking back on all those times when I was a child and mistaken for a boy and felt devastated, I want to hug that little girl and tell her that she's normal. I want to tell her that gender is fluid. I want to tell her that someday she'll be all right. That someday she will be a role model for a little kid who doesn't quite fit in. And that she will grow up to be happy.

***

I was always gender queer, but at a certain age I began to put the masculine part of me away, and I got depressed. Now, I dress however I want to and wear what I consider a masculine chain with a heavy dog tag attached to it, etched with the Hebrew word for "life," *chai*. I'm beginning to feel more like myself every day.

I think it's interesting that when I was young, I was embarrassed when people misgendered me as a boy, but today, I am annoyed when people refer to me as "she," or refer to my girlfriend and me as "ladies." I yelled at a waiter recently for doing just that. I even stopped attending all-women Twelve-Step meetings. I just don't feel like a woman anymore. Maybe I never did. And being misgendered as female triggers me so that I re-experience all the pain I felt when I was misgendered as a kid. This is one of the reasons I decided to take testosterone. If I look more masculine, I won't be misgendered anymore, and maybe I won't have to feel that pain anymore.

***

When I was recovering from cancer two years ago, I spent a lot of time meditating. After many hours of pondering what I wanted to do with the rest of my life, I started thinking about who I really was. At my core, who am I? I am that same little girl who wanted to be masculine.

I still don't know if I'm a trans man; but I do know I'm what's called "trans masculine." That means I was assigned female at birth but identify as masculine. I changed my pronouns to "they/them" and asked my closest friends to start calling me "Eli," short for "*Elisha*," my Hebrew name. I slowly enlarged the circle of people who knew me as Eli until all that was left were my colleagues at work. I hesitated for a few weeks. How would they react? Would they think less of me? And then I thought, "Who the hell cares?" I needed to be my authentic self in all the parts of my life. I sent my colleagues an email and told Human Resources to change my name. The next week, I got a new email address. No one so much as batted an eye.

I am now Eli to all who know me. When I meet someone, I introduce myself that way. My current partner only knows me as Eli, and when she uses the name, I feel a sense of joy and pride.

Maybe my parents knew something when I was born. Maybe God told them to name me Elisha. Maybe I was meant to be "Eli" all along.

***

I tried to let out my real self over the years, little by little. I came out as a lesbian at twenty-six. I chopped off my hair at twenty-nine. I wore men's clothing on and off for most of my life.

The transformation into my truest self still wasn't quite complete, though. When I got divorced, I legally changed my name to Eli Michael Klyde. Michael was my grandfather's name. I am named for him—Lynn Michelle for Michael Lee—so I think Eli Michael is appropriate. My Hebrew name is now *Elisha Maor. Maor* means "one who brings light," and that's what I try to do as a professor.

If we are indeed created *B'tzelem Elohim*–in the image of God–then I need to celebrate that creation.

It took me fifty-five years, a lot of suffering, and too many teardrops to find my true self. More importantly, it took me that long to finally be okay with myself. To realize there was nothing wrong with me. That I was good enough. That Eli was good enough.

It wasn't until I got sober that I totally accepted my gender-queer self. I was filled with shame for so long, trying to drink away the pain. And it's not like my family would have thrown me out if they knew the truth. They accepted me at seven, wearing a suit and a kippah at my brother's Bar Mitzvah. *I* was the one who couldn't accept the truth. *I* was the one who had to be convinced that there was worth inside of me.

I finally love the person I've become.

I envy today's youngsters who come out in high school, or even sooner, like those who know they are transgender in kindergarten. Why did it take me so long? Did I need to make this difficult journey, just so the ending would taste sweeter? Was all the pain worth it? That seems a bit harsh—like something my parents would have told me. But maybe it's true.

Or maybe I just want young people who read this book to have an easier life than I did. Maybe I just want them to know that it gets better. That they don't need to fit society's expectations. That it's perfectly okay to make other people a little uncomfortable once in a while. That no one can tell them who they are. That they must figure that out for themselves. That they are, indeed, good enough.

Me and my son at his Bar Mitzvah party in 2018.

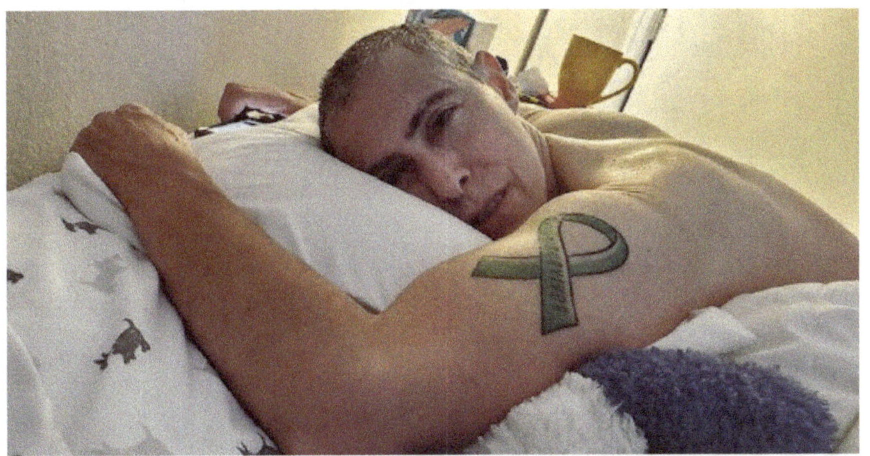

Me in 2024, showing off my survivor tattoo.

Me at a Red Sox-Rockies game in 2024 at Coors Field.